Principles to Propel South Sudan Forward

Stephen Mathiang

A Note from the Publisher

The publisher wishes to acknowledge and thank Dr Douglas H. Johnson for his invaluable help and support for Africa World Books and its mission of preserving and promoting African cultural and literary traditions and history. Dr Johnson and fellow historians have been instrumental in ensuring that African people remain connected to their past and their identity. Africa World Books is proud to carry on this mission.

© Stephen Mathiang, 2015

ISBN: 978-0-6453010-9-0

Cover design, typesetting and layout : Africa World Books

Contents

Dedication

First, I wholeheartedly dedicate this book to all South Sudanese people and their national leaders.

Second, I sincerely dedicate this book to all human rights activists, advocates of good governance and all godly people.

Last, but not the least, I honestly dedicate it to all other people who have the interest of their families, societies, nations and the entire world at heart.

Acknowledgements

My appreciation goes to my diligent editor, Wilson N. Macharia, who polished and made this book a captivating read.

It will be very unfair for me to end here without expressing merited thanks to my dear wife Elizabeth Agot Leek and my children, Ajoh, Kuch, Alier, Jogaak and Areu and my nephew Kuch Bech, who are always by my side as I journey along the lonely path in the artistic and creative world.

Preface

I have been thinking deeply about the future of my nation of South Sudan since I came to know the difference between a peaceful, well-established country and one with a poor foundation. As I wrestled with my thoughts and drew heavily from my life experiences, I realized that a nation is shaped and guided along the path of its growth and development by the cultural values of her peoples and by the way she responds to her dynamic environments.

If people cherish love, honesty, kindness, fear of God, hard work, respect for human life and other forms of desirable human behaviour, their nation will have a good foundation and see prosperity. In such a nation where people are guided by noble principles, citizens love and respect each other, share their national resources equally and equitably, work and live peacefully in unity. In such an environment, people make, own and manage the government for their common good. Good governance is the cornerstone of the country.

On the other hand, when the people of the

land embrace even a little bit of ethical deviance, not minding to practise dishonesty, hatred, jealousy, envy, selfishness and the like, their nation suffers as a result of these wrong values. Such a country gets riddled with corruption, as a result of which people fight over national resources, viewing each other as potential enemies. The future of such a country is bleak.

But experience has shown that every culture contains a mixture of good and undesirable aspects. There is no culture that is a hundred per cent good or a hundred per cent bad. Culture is also never static. As such, people must keep modifying and improving on their culture by eliminating wrong aspects of it and replacing them with good ones. That way they make it relevant and easy to integrate with other cultures.

The purpose of this book is to offer insights on how South Sudanese people can modify and improve their cultures for synergy so that they end up with a strong national culture that is guided by sound ethical principles. These principles will help people establish their good, enduring national foundation and will also in turn inform the crafting of sound national policies that will steer the Republic of South Sudan along the rough path of her growth and development. You and I are the face of our young nation, and it is by the way outsiders see us that they will judge our nation.

Stephen Mathiang

General
Introduction

If you really wish to establish yourself, your family, your community, your country or your world on a solid, moral foundation, this book is for you. Although it is primarily targeted at the people of the young Republic of South Sudan and their government, what it teaches has a universal application and could benefit people in any society.

People have a moral choice to build a nation that is well-founded or one that is established on wrong values. The citizens are the ones who build a great nation, and they do it on purpose by embracing acceptable ethical principles. In her case, South Sudan has chosen to be guided by "justice", "liberty" and "prosperity". Currently, these are the principles that are supposed to inform the policies of this nation. In order to strengthen these core values for the building of national foundation, I propose we add "equality", "fear" and "love" so that our nation starts to be guided by six core values. These are just my personal suggestions. But I am persuaded that if we are determined to seek justice for all, liberty for all, prosperity for all, equality for all, fear and love of God, and love for one another, we will end up enriching our national policies and come up with government plans that help make all of us benefit from our young nation. These values are the enduring ingredients of good governance. Chapter One of this book explores the essence of good national foundation and core values.

National resources can be a blessing or a curse, depending on how they are exploited and utilised. For instance, if their exploitation and utilisation is guided by good ethical principles like love, integrity, transparency and accountability, the resources will benefit all the citizens of the nation, thus making them a national blessing. But if their exploitation and utilisation is guided by selfishness and greed, the national resources will benefit only a few citizens. This will engender conflict as people fight to get their share of the national cake and end up derailing the nation from its path of growth and development. That way the resources, no matter how vast they are, become a national curse. Chapter Two discusses the different ways by which we can make our vast national wealth a blessing.

There has been rumour of widespread corruption in our young nation of South Sudan, although I don't know whether what is being said can be substantiated. To me, if this financial scandal is not handled well, it will destabilise our young nation and rift our citizens apart. So for us to benefit from the lost funds, to unite our people and stabilise our nation, I personally suggest that we forgive those who might have exploited our resources and stashed funds emanating thereof abroad. Then we ask them to return and invest the funds locally to boost our national economy. The war we should be fighting now is that of putting in place structures that will facilitate good governance and requiring that they be followed.

By and large, Arabic and English are spoken in the urban areas, as a result of which most of our rural folks feel side-lined. Seventy-six per cent of our people are illiterate, with female illiteracy in our nation being the highest in the world. It is imperative that we make identifying a national language that most people can use to communicate and dealing with the high illiteracy rate a priority. This is the subject of Chapter Three, wherein I have also attempted to flesh out possible solutions to these critical issues. Also discussed in this chapter is the above-mentioned financial scandal.

In chapter four, I briefly explain how South Sudanese have had no actual unity among themselves before they obtained their national independence in 2011. I also shed light on how the current decentralization system of the government enhances or facilitates the disunity of the people, for people have to unite first before they seek to decentralize themselves if they so wished. Then I propose ways to slow down the quest about decentralization system and promote national unity instead. Discussed in this chapter too is the importance of unity among our people, despite their diversity.

A nation earns admiration if her people are known for espousing acceptable moral principles. With this awareness, I have devoted the last chapter of the book to exploring the core values that I feel should inform the morality of our nation and make our country esteemed. These include, respect for senior and disabled citizens, respect for national leaders, respect for women and youths, respect for all armed forces, respect for widows and orphans, respect for single ladies, respect for national wealth, respect for aliens, respect for national law, government and politics. On top of all these should be a healthy self-respect, a vital but missing link in our individual and national dignity. Also parts of what I believe to be the roots of our national self-esteem are equitable distribution of the national cake, national tolerance and forgiveness, religious pluralism and tolerance, good neighbourliness, maximisation of friends and minimisation of enemies. Lastly, I have discussed in the same chapter the importance of protecting national environment.

I know our founding leaders have been doing whatever they can to put our young nation of South Sudan on a solid foundation to grow and develop as a strong, respected nation in the global community of nations. Indeed, some of the noble principles that I suggest in this book have been used in drafting the national constitution and in major policy documents.

The role of this book is to restate their importance and advance further suggestions to make our nation viable and strong. Please read and study it, and you will never regret having had it now in your hands.

Chapter One

THE IMPORTANCE OF A GOOD FOUNDATION AND NATIONAL CORE VALUES

Introduction

This chapter explores the importance of a good national foundation that is informed by core values like moral purity, integrity and love. These are the basis of a strong, durable nation. A nation founded on them will weather any socio-economic and political upheavals.

The other kind of nation is one with a poor foundation that is characterised by bad values such as injustice, dishonesty, selfishness, hatred, jealousy, etc. A nation that promotes such moral corruption can be compared to a building standing on sandy ground, and it is sure to crash when faced with adverse circumstances.

The building of a strong foundation is a prerequisite for any nation's success. Hence, it is incumbent on all the people of South Sudan to establish an enduring national foundation if their young republic is to have a good future.

Just like individuals, every nation must go through difficult times in her history, and good core values are what sustain it along the rough path of her growth and development. In order to safeguard the national image and guarantee the achievement of the national vision and individual aspirations, people should adhere to their national code of ethics. In the case of South Sudan, we aspire for justice for all, liberty for all, prosperity for all, equality for all, fear and love of God and sincere love for one another.

The Importance of a Good Foundation

It is common knowledge that the way a building looks like depends on its foundation. That is, the stronger the foundation, the stronger the building; the weaker the foundation, the weaker the building. Accordingly, a building that is intended to have many floors must have a deeper and stronger foundation than a low-rise building. The same case applies to trees. Tall trees usually have longer roots for stability.

In Matthew 7:24-27, Jesus Christ teaches about two builders: one wise, and the other one foolish. The wise one lays the foundation of his house on a solid rock, and when the wind and rain comes, his dwelling is not shaken. But that is not so with the foolish builder. The latter, seemingly avoiding the hassle of digging hard ground, makes the foundation of his building on sand. When it rains heavily, the streams rise and the wind blows terribly, this house is brought down with a thud.

Jesus Christ uses this parable on building to illustrate the fact that people's fate depends on how they respond to His life-changing Word. There is hope for a bright future for the person who pays heed and acts on what Jesus says, but there is hopelessness for the careless person who merely hears but does not act upon the Word of the Lord.

Jesus Christ metaphorically uses the rain, wind and stream to illustrate the various types of trials and challenges that we humans contend with daily. These include physiological needs and feelings of insecurity that Satan uses to turn people away from their Creator. Thus, it is imperative that a Christian consistently keeps his faith anchored in the Lord Jesus through the help of the Holy Spirit in order to have a harmonious and growing personal relationship with God.

But can Jesus' wise illustration be related to building a nation? The answer is "yes". It is one thing to build a nation, but building a nation that will endure difficult times and sustain her effort at development is another thing. But how can people build their nation on a solid rock and not on a sandy foundation?

Building a strong, durable nation is not always an easy task. The reason many nations of the world are currently torn apart by strife is because of being built on a shaky ground. Very often when a nation gets independence, her founding leaders set it on a wrong path, in most cases unknowingly. This mainly happens when they put it on the rough path of development without first laying a good foundation. They tend to be in a hurry because of two reasons: first, they desire to have their young nation develop quickly until it catches up with developed nations, not knowing that such nations took a long time to get to where they are. Second, the leaders of the young nation think that the quicker their nation develops the faster they become rich. But time is a factor that cannot be ignored so far as development is concerned, and if you rush development, the little progress you had made may give in to regression, and eventually the nation collapses.

I am reminded of certain poorly built houses whose owners, driven by pride and financial gains, put them up in a hurry, compromising the quality of their foundations and other vital considerations. Unfortunately, such buildings end up collapsing and destroying the lives of innocent people. I say "innocent people" because the owners of these rickety structures are rarely the ones trapped in them when they cave in. And like these greedy landlords who very often escape the consequences of their action, greedy leaders often get away with their ill-gotten wealth when their poorly founded countries sink into chaos and leave the innocent citizens suffering.

As in the case of putting up a good house, laying down a proper, strong and deep foundation is a must when building a nation. Surviving the rough, long path of national development without such a solid foundation is impossible. Therefore, people should be patient no matter how long it takes to establish this concrete foundation, for this is a key factor for the success of a nation.

People base the foundation of their nation on principles of their own choice. These principles are, for instance, justice, equality, unity, freedom of speech and association, gender equality, human rights, etc. In their case, theocratic states base the foundation of their countries on key religious principles. But very often, the major challenge comes when people begin to match their chosen national principles with action—living out these ideals. Documenting principles by which to live may be easy; the hard part is implementing them, one reason being lack of seriousness on the part of national leaders. They are the ones who are supposed to lead in implementing what they put down on paper.

If such principles are to take root, first, they must be in harmony with the common people's aspirations; indeed, they should contribute towards promoting and protecting them. The moment people are happy with them, they will cherish, uphold and protect the principles. This means that even leaders and others who work for the government will also cherish, uphold and safeguard them. Second, there should be a just law in place that specifies penalties to be applied against those who deliberately flout these principles and serve as a deterrent to others. This law will be applied fairly in enforcing the national principles for the betterment of all citizens.

As already established, a good national foundation is informed by good moral principles, whereas poor ethical values lead to a bad foundation. For the current and future generations of South Sudanese to develop and play their role in the global community effectively, we and our leaders must diligently and sacrificially contribute to building our nation and do it on a firm foundation. If we take comfort in living in a rickety structure and continue enjoying ourselves without doing something about it, the building will collapse upon us, and we will be the ones to blame.

National Core Values

In this section, I wish to highlight the importance of our national core values. The founders of our nation chose "justice", "liberty" and "prosperity" and enshrined them to inform our policies that would in turn guide the nation towards achieving her vision. They influence how the nation deals with her internal affairs as well how it deals with her external environment. But I feel we should add three core values, namely, "equality", "fear" and "love". In my opinion—which I feel I am entitled to in line with the freedom of expression— our country would benefit more should it be guided by these six basic principles. The reasons why I suggest the inclusion of the last three values will become clear in the following section where I explore the benefits of each principle.

Justice

People should be dealt with fairly, irrespective of their socio-economic, political, ethnic, religious and geographic backgrounds. Justice refers to fairness in the manner people are dealt with; it is one of the key components of moral purity. The founding leaders of South Sudan declared war with the Khartoum government in pursuant of justice; therefore, it was only natural to make justice a key principle for informing policies crafted to guide the new nation.

The founding leaders of South Sudan achieved their noble goal of justice for their people upon the historical declaration of the independence of their nation on 9 July, 2011. Henceforth, the relationship between South Sudan and Sudan changed. Both countries are viewed as sovereign in the eyes of the global community of nations.

But in order for this core value not to remain as an empty national slogan, it is incumbent on our people and their government to be intentional to "Let justice roll on like a river, righteousness like a never-falling stream!" (Amos 5:24). Justice is what we fought and died for, so we are to cherish, uphold, safeguard and practise it within and outside our national borders. It should govern the distribution of social services, development of national infrastructure, employment opportunities, political activities, economic development and access to justice, among others, to all citizens and regions. Let justice be for all in South Sudan. Let us not die for what our beloved freedom fighters died for and won!

Liberty

Liberty means the freedom to live as you wish or go where you want. For most people, it also means the freedom to exercise religious or political beliefs of one's choice. Liberty is another significant national core value in South Sudan.

Although SPLA/SPLM was established to wage a war of liberation against Khartoum government, liberty came to have additional meaning to our people. They came to see it as freedom from all sorts of bondage, particularly the oppression by fellow men. After a long bloody struggle, political freedom was realised by the South Sudanese people on 9 July 2011 when South Sudan got her independence from Sudan.

If political independence was the only cause of war, then the word "liberty" would have lost its real meaning to us. But it means freedom from other bondages such as hunger and poverty, illiteracy and ignorance, disease, corruption, insecurity and tribalism as well. Therefore, emancipation from Sudan is not the end to our fight for liberty. It is the beginning of a long, tricky journey towards greater liberty for the South Sudanese. Our people are bogged down by numerous challenges that have been with them for many centuries and are still weighing them down even now.

National programmes should be guided by the desire to liberate people from the different burdens that have been weighing them down. Let the fight for liberty continue for the common good of our people. It is common knowledge that actions speak more than words; so we must purposely ensure that everybody in our nation reaps the benefit of this core value.

Prosperity

Prosperity is the state of being successful, having a lot of money. In a prosperous nation, no one should go hungry. Prosperity is an important driving core value in South Sudan.

In the old Sudan, some people, especially in the south of the country, were greatly disadvantaged materially. Hence, the founders of the SPLA/SPLM enshrined this moral motto in the revolutionary manifesto that there be proper exploitation of all national resources to make the entire nation rich. Of course, when the country becomes richer, her individual people become richer, too.

At this early stage of the birth of the South Sudan noticeable prosperity is yet to be realized; less than 0.04% of the population can be said to have experienced some form of prosperity. As for how or where they got their wealth, they alone and their God know.

Prosperous people love one another and generally live in peace, but when the term becomes the experience of a few, the result is hatred, envy and animosity among the people. If we talk of prosperity for all, then there must be concerted effort at all levels of government to make the whole nation and her people prosperous.

Equality

Equality means viewing people of diverse backgrounds as equal and treating them as so. We must aspire for equality if we are to strengthen our moral core values and achieve parity in the distribution of national resources so as to create a harmonious relationship among our citizens.

Everything possible should be done to make all our citizens feel that they are participating in the political process on an equal footing and that they are getting their fair share of the national cake and other benefits enjoyed by those who belong in a sovereign nation. There should be gender equality as well so that males and females are regarded equally. Equality should be considered when budgeting for physical infrastructure and other developmental aspects as well. Even in courts of justice, equality should be observed to ensure that all citizens receive justice as provided in the constitution. On both regional and international scene, South Sudan values and expects to have mutual relationships between her and other nations.

But we have a long way to go before we manage to give equality an opportunity to completely annihilate inequality and have a South Sudan where all people have quenched their moral thirst. This is because the genuine essence of equality has not yet been felt by all our people, and the road to its actual realization is proving to be bumpy. Yet it is too early for anyone to blame the government for not permitting equality triumph among its citizens, for the nation is still in the process of developing the necessary structures that will facilitate development. What is needed at this stage, though, is the willingness and desire from the national leaders to translate this national principle into reality for the goodness of all.

Fear

Ordinarily, fear refers to an undesirable emotion or thought that you have when you are frightened or worried that something dangerous, painful or bad might happen. But fear may be healthy if it prevents you from doing something that you know to be morally bad, as a result of which you change and begin practising what is morally good. For instance, the reverential fear of God will make you to respect God and relate well with your fellow human beings. Indeed, King Solomon says, "The fear of the Lord is the beginning of knowledge, but fools despise wisdom and discipline" (Prov 1:7).

If we fear God, we will not do or say what he does not like; instead, we will strive to do his bidding and say what he likes. We will also embrace and practise good moral values while shunning what is evil. Fear of God will also impress on us the need to view each other as being created in the image and likeness of God and therefore, worthy of humane treatment.

Being guided by the fear of God will help the South Sudanese people and their government to exercise other core values wisely for the goodness of all and for God's glory as well. In return, the Lord will bestow his abundant blessings upon our land.

Love

What I am referring to here is that selfless and sacrificial love called "agape". In place of self-gratification, this kind of love focuses on pleasing others and meeting their needs. This kind of love is also a morally binding factor.

South Sudan's guiding principles—justice, liberty, prosperity, equality, and fear of God—are good, but they need genuine love to glue them together. Without love as a binding factor, these principles and other moral ingredients will remain mere aspirations. Nothing that is intended to help people can bear fruit unless it is viewed and done with love. That is why Jesus Christ's second great commandment is, 'Love your neighbour as yourself' (Matt.22:39).

If you really loved your neighbour as yourself, you would do to him what you would like him to do to you. Love will compel you to fulfil all the Ten Commandments. For example, if you love your father and mother as yourself, you will honour them. If you really love your neighbour as yourself, you will not kill him. If you really love your neighbour as yourself, you will not commit adultery with his spouse. If you really love your neighbour as yourself, you will not steal from him. If you truly love your neighbour as yourself, you will not give false testimony against him. If you actually love your neighbour as yourself, you will not covet his wife or her husband. Nor will you set your heart on his house, land or any other thing that belongs to him if you love him as yourself.

If we really love our fellow South Sudanese neighbours as ourselves, we should help them have access to justice, assist them to be liberated from their burdens of life, help them to prosper like us, honour their human rights and help them access their national benefits, help them to enjoy equal social and other benefits like all other national citizens and do to them things that are in line with God's will.

Genuine love for God and other people ought to be the main root that firmly upholds and drives the Republic of South Sudan along her path of development. If we are to laugh and cry together in our young nation, there must be justice for all, liberty for all, prosperity for all, equality for all, fear and love of God and respect for other human beings in and outside South Sudan.

Summary

Since the nation belongs to all of us South Sudanese, we, males and females, young and old, have the inescapable duty to slow down our search for riches and focus more on building a proper foundation for our country. This national foundation involves the establishment of acceptable, respectable, strong and enduring rule of law that can guide the nation along the path of growth and development. To me, the role of our current post-independence generation is to build a formidable national foundation upon which the next generations will build as they take our nation of South Sudan to greater heights of prosperity. Our primary concern should not be on how long it takes to build this foundation but rather how we are to lay down the best national foundation for the benefit of the present and future generations. Trees with the most valuable wood take time to grow. Accordingly, let us tighten our belts and sweat now as we protect the valuable inheritance of our children's children and ensure that they enjoy life in future.

If you agree with me that our national core values should be justice, liberty, prosperity, equality, fear and love, then it is our moral duty to cherish, uphold and protect them. These values should guide our people's thinking, actions and words; they are to govern her people's behaviour as they relate to one another, as they govern themselves, as they relate to their neighbours, and as they relate to their Creator. Good moral values produce good people and, accordingly, good nations. Let us live out our beliefs.

Chapter Two

NATIONAL WEALTH—A CURSE OR A BLESSING?

Introduction

My people teach that the things that are of value to you are also the source of your problems. For instance, your intelligence is your problem; your water pool is your problem; your wealth is your problem; your beautiful daughter or handsome son is your problem; your beautiful wife or handsome husband is your problem. The reason these things are problems is because other people would also want to have them.

Based on the above argument, what immediately comes to your mind when you think of the wealth of the young nation of South Sudan? Is it possible for her vast wealth to be a curse? I want you to keep these two questions in your mind as we consider the vast resources of South Sudan.

This chapter centres on the major sources of our national and personal revenues, which include the land, the waters, agricultural products, minerals, income from tourism, customs and immigration fees, tax, income from games and sports, art, music and foreign aid. If the proceeds from these sources of income were to be utilised in accordance with our national core values—justice for all, liberty for all, prosperity for all, equality for all, fear and love of God and sincere love for one another—then they would be a blessing for the whole nation and her people. But if their exploitation is driven by greed, selfishness, hatred, jealousy, envy, disunity and other vices, the nation would be better without them. Please join me as I briefly examine the value of land here.

The Value of Land

As is clear from the map of Africa, the Republic of South Sudan is landlocked, being a bridge between North and East Africa. It borders Ethiopia to the east, Kenya to the southeast, Uganda to the south, the Democratic Republic of the Congo to the southwest, the Central Africa Republic to the west, and Sudan to the north. Her total area is 644,329 sq. km.

The total length of national boundaries is about 5,413 km, which can be broken-down as follows: boundary with Central African Republic, 989 km; boundary with Democratic Republic of the Congo, 639 km; boundary with Ethiopia, 934 km; boundary with Kenya, 232 km; boundary with Uganda, 435 km, and boundary with Sudan, 2,184 km. Yet it is important to mention that the South Sudan-Sudan border represents the status as on 1 January 1956. The two nations are yet to come to a consensus in respect of their frontier following the declaration of South Sudan's independence from Sudan. The status of Abyei is also still unresolved.

White Nile, the biggest and longest river, traverses this country from the south to the north. And there are still many smaller rivers in this nation. The terrain includes tropical forests, swamps and rich savannah grasslands. The Sudd, Bahr el Ghazal and Sobat rivers traverse long stretches of swamps.

As you fly over or drive through South Sudan, you notice that most of the land is still uninhabited. Population is concentrated along major roads and urban areas where people have access to social services provided by the government and other humanitarian and development actors.

At the time of my writing, our country's stood at 11,562,695 people. That means that if we divided this land equally among its own citizens, every person would have 13.77 acres. Accordingly, if South Sudan fairly and thoroughly implements her six core values of justice for all, liberty for all, prosperity for all, equality for all, fear and love of God and sincere love for each other, there would be no landless people among her citizens for centuries to come. And this is so despite the fact that the government now owns and will continue claiming some land for use in providing communal services, roads and agricultural schemes to ensure our people have food to eat. Some foreign and national agricultural projects will also claim some share of the national land to execute their activities. Still another part of the land will go towards building industries and other necessary development activities.

Yet if the motto of our national founders was to have a South Sudan where there would be no landless people, then the national land policy should prohibit unnecessary taking away of land from its original owners. And whenever any part of the land is leased to any individuals or agency, it should also directly or indirectly benefit the indigenous people either through employment or other verifiable ways.

As I write, it is very unfortunate that some South Sudanese have lost and others are losing their precious lives over endless land issues. Of course, they have the right to fight—even if it meant losing life as they do so—to recover their ancestral land if it has been unlawfully occupied. But to me, given the vastness of the land with which the South Sudanese people are blessed, I feel that less costly approaches should be employed because the life of any South Sudanese man or woman, old or young, rich or poor, is still more valuable than any piece of land that has been occupied illegally. If we really love each other as ourselves and sincerely comply with our national core values, we should be ready to share equally our land resources, be it grazing area, water source or farming zone, and this would lead to greater joy and peace among us.

But if we don't change our current selfish attitude, our people will lead an unfulfilling life that is characterized by self-centredness where people delight in being from Dinkaland, Nuerland, Murleland, Zandeland, Shiilukland, Bariland, Taposaland, Latukoland, Abyeiland and Anyuakland, among others, rather than being South Sudanese. This will have the effect of having a nation that is not united because whenever any of these "motherlands" is attacked or threatened by external force, the rest of the people will go on with their life, seeing that as a mere distant thunder that produces no rain. Consequently, these divided people will be regrettably defeated and sooner or later, their land either taken away or their resources totally exploited by external forces. For those who are not aware, these are some of the negative consequences of disunity. That is why the Americans say: "Divided we fall, united we stand."

I gather that because of greed, ignorance and other moral ills, our people are now indirectly selling precious pieces of real estate through misguided land leasing. Some naïve citizens, I am told, are leasing their land to wealthy aliens for as long as one hundred years. My question is: Why are we depriving our children and children's children of their motherland? Should we continue to live as tenants in our land, especially in our own urban centres? True, the title deed of your land is in your name, and you have an inalienable right to do whatever you like with it. But you should know that your parcel of land is part of a bigger parcel of land, the nation of South Sudan that our national martyrs shed their blood over.

Please get me right! I am not saying that an individual, a community or an agency has no right to own and manage a specific piece of land as they choose; rather, what I am saying is that when it comes to long-term land leasing, the government ought to be involved in the deal to safeguard national interests. What do you want to do with your money when you don't have the land? Another negative effect of land leasing is that it will lead to prolonged idleness of some of our people. That is, if they are promised regular payment, why would they bother to work?

I desperately long to see a South Sudan where all citizens are totally free, and people are welcomed to acquire and possess property, live, work, die and be buried anywhere within the four corners of their nation. Then people will not be necessarily identified with their ethnic group but with the towns or regions they live in. Hence, their political constituencies will automatically consist of a good combination of national citizens from different tribes. In hiring people to work for the government, the guiding factor will be "putting the right person in the right place" instead of the old notion of seeking tribal representation. Over time, tribal feuds will give way to good neighbourliness. Just like Martin Luther wanted concerning America, we should strive for the day when South Sudanese people "will not be judged by the color of their skin, but by the content of their character", the day when our people will not be judged by their mother tongue but by their individual behaviour. For example, if I, the author of this book, am morally depraved, that is not because I am a Dinka; it is because I have chosen to be so as an individual. True, Dinka culture may have some influence over my life, but that does not warrant someone to make a blanket statement that the way I behave is representative of the way Dinkas behave. Like people of other ethnic groups, Dinkas are not identical in character, for they don't all act, think and talk in the same way. I don't think even the so-called identical twins behave the same in every way.

If we love each other as ourselves, if we all own some land, if we all benefit from the land, we will all be engaged in protecting our nation and will be ready to die for it together should it be faced with external threat. This is the real essence of national unity. If not so, for us Christians, Jesus Christ's second coming will find us, we South Sudanese people, still engaged in a useless war over the beautiful land without benefitting from it. Let our land be a blessing to all of us, not a curse. Now join me in the following section in exploring other major sources of our national and individual income.

Other Major Sources of the Nation's Revenue

The Republic of South Sudan is rich, being endowed with abundant natural resources. There is a common, metaphorical saying that is still in use in the old Sudan that if you drop down a nail in South Sudan, it will germinate. There is undeniable truth in this saying if you consider the vast arable land with its immense wealth above and beneath it. These riches are untapped and too numerous to quantify. Indeed, any type of business undertaking in South Sudan is sure to succeed. In the next section, I have broken down and discussed our national wealth under different subheadings.

Water Resources

In January 2014, Hon. Maker Chol Adol and I together with other passengers sailed the Nile by motor boat from Bor to Awierial County. Being my first time to take such a trip, I greatly awed by the vastness of the Nile and its rich vegetation. This provoked me to ask Maker, "Are our warring people aware of the beautiful land that they are busy destroying instead of developing?" Surprised like me, he just shook his head.

If properly utilized, our country's rivers, particularly the Nile with its vast Sudd swamps, have the potential to make South Sudan wealthier than any nation under the sun. The waters from the Nile and its tributaries are fresh and good for general consumption.

Fishery

Now let us briefly consider the value of fishery of the Nile and its tributaries. The Sudd covers an estimated 30,000 sq. km. It is estimated that the Sudd area has the potential of producing about 300,000 metric tons of fish per year. These include tilapia, Nile perch and catfish. Smaller rivers too abound with varieties of fish and provide fishing opportunities throughout the year.

If fishing is done well and the products managed in a way that meets international standards, the result will be revenue in foreign currency for the nation and income that will raise the standard of living for individuals. Fishing business will create employment opportunities for many who live along these rivers and the entire nation in general. The other benefit is that when fish finds its way into our people's diet, their health will improve.

Hydroelectric power

The nation could use her very reliable water resource to produce hydroelectric power for the whole nation's needs and even export it to the neighbouring countries. And the place to start generating power would be Fula Fall near Nimule. Generating power should be a national priority since the nation greatly needs electricity to power industries and for lighting in homes. Hydroelectric power would drastically reduce today's many huge and expensive foreign generators that are, after all, unreliable. The moment people and industries become hooked to less expensive electric power, the cheaper the locally produced goods become and accordingly, the lower the cost of living. This project will generate job opportunities locally and nationally.

Consumption

Water sources in South Sudan have the potential of meeting the nation's domestic demand for water. The availability of many sources of fresh water is what makes South Sudan to have a high population of different wildlife species, for they easily get drinking water. These water sources sustain a large number of animals in South Sudan because there is plenty of drinking water and grazing lands for them. The vast swamps along the Nile are home to all sorts of birds and animals that live in water. These include crocodiles, hippopotamus, etc.

For domestic use and drinking, people depend mainly on waters from the Nile and its tributaries. Before water filtration became common, and even now in some places, locals drink water in its raw form, despite the seriousness of water-borne diseases. As I write now, these huge water resources are supporting thriving and profitable water purification enterprises. These businesses have created numerous job opportunities for the South Sudanese and even foreigners.

Farming

The frontages of these rivers and the swamps that they create have proven to be good agricultural land, supporting large- and- small-scale farming. During dry seasons, people grow maize, sugarcane and a variety of vegetables as the water level recedes. In most cases, farmers do not water their farms because the soil is still wet enough to support the growing of crops. But even when it is dry, the rivers have enough water to support irrigation systems.

The silt that these rivers have been depositing along their banks from time immemorial makes agriculture in such areas possible even without the use of fertilisers. And of course, food grown without fertilisers has proven to be healthier; so the health of our people is greatly improved. These natural food products attract foreigners as well, becoming a source of foreign currency and thus, a booster to the local and national economy.

In this area there is potential for many job opportunities for our people, although we need also to strike a balance when exploiting these resources so that we do not deprive our domestic and wild animals of water.

Transport and Tourism

The major rivers provide reliable mode of transport in

the nation, especially to those living along their banks. For example, big steamers and motorboats as well as dugout canoes use the Nile between Juba and Renk for much-needed public and private transport. River transport conveys bulky goods easily between the various ports.

In addition, the rivers, especially the Nile, attract local and international tourists, which results in huge income both to the locals and the nation at large. Consequently, our local and national governments need to pay special, urgent attention to this important source of income and invest heavily in exploiting and protecting it. It has the potential of creating many job opportunities for our nationals.

Plant Factory

Certain plants like papyrus that grow along these rivers can be exploited economically. For example, a paper factory that could produce paper products for both local consumption and export ought to be set up in the swampy regions. This is another area the government could explore in an effort to look for employment for our citizens.

Ecological Balance

South Sudan experiences sufficient rainfall annually. A lot of evaporation takes place in the Nile and its tributaries, eventually leading to rainfall. That is, the water evaporates, form clouds in the air which then fall to the ground as rain. These rivers are really one of our greatest blessings.

Problem with the Waters

We have already seen some of our blessings in form of huge natural waters. But the negative side of these waters becomes visible when they are selfishly managed and controlled with ethnic interests in mind, with those near them exploiting them with utter disregard for the rest of the people who depend on them.

Our wild animals, despite being numerous, don't experience any lack of water because they have equal access to water sources. The problem of water is brought about by fellow human beings, especially pastoralists. Those who live next to the water sources tend to monopolize the commodity by disregarding fellow countrymen who live far away from the rivers. Even those living near the rivers sometimes quarrel among themselves over water when it is not equitably shared.

What those who live far away from the water sources ask for is to have unhindered access to water for themselves and their domestic animals. If their request is lovingly granted, they enjoy the waters and grazing lands with their animals during dry season until the onset of the rainy season. Thereafter, they move back to their own settlements and do the same in the next dry period. In this way, the two communities build a good relationship between themselves and trust each other. They share their natural resources mutually in love and safeguard and protect them together whenever they are threatened.

But when their request is not honoured, they tend to take the law into their own hands by trying to access the water sources by force, for to them, this is a matter of life or death. As a result, those who claimed ownership of the water sources feel that their rights are being violated and arm themselves to try to fight back the invaders. This is a normal occurrence now in South Sudan, which often leads to loss of innocent lives, destruction of property, cattle rustling, disunity among the citizens and threat to national security, among other challenges.

At the regional level, Nile waters benefit many nations bordering South Sudan and those that are beyond, including Egypt. People say, "Egypt is the Nile, and the Nile is Egypt." This is simply because the country entirely depends on the Nile waters for all its domestic uses as well as its extensive irrigation systems that support the country's agricultural activities.

Since 1891, the usage of the Nile waters has been subject to constant political negotiations, resulting in numerous regional Nile water agreements involving the present ten countries of Burundi, Rwanda, Tanzania, Kenya, Uganda, Congo (DRC), South Sudan, Sudan, Ethiopia and Eretria.

It is the serious demand of the Nile waters by Egypt that led to the unfinished digging of the Jonglei Canal project. The aim was to convey more water to Egypt, since some people felt a lot of water was getting lost in the Sudd and other swampy regions inside South Sudan. If this canal project was successfully completed, it would have resulted in two opposing consequences, one negative and one positive. On the negative side, South Sudan would have lost most of the benefits that come with the waters of the Nile. On the positive side, the amount of water that gets to Egypt would have increased dramatically. This would have enhanced Egypt's agriculture and other activities that depend on water.

In order to avoid any national or regional conflict over the usage of the Nile waters, South Sudan should amend its existing laws and policies governing the management and usage of this essential commodity. Doing this would need to be guided by our national principles—justice for all, liberty for all, prosperity for all, equality for all, fear and love of God as well as love for one another—so that the new laws and policies be for the common good of all. Else, the Nile waters will be a national curse instead of blessing.

Agricultural Benefits

When I first went to the USA on a short visit in 2003, I was highly impressed by many of that nation's achievements. But there is one specific thing among these important achievements I can't forget: managing to defeat hunger through an effective food security system. It really amazed me that the government took care of the essential needs of even the so-called homeless people. I believe the founders of that nation took hunger as the number one enemy. Thus, they fought hard against it until they annihilated it. Well-fed people look healthy and are able to think and come up with ideas that improve the welfare of the nation.

Why was I so impressed by the fact that people in the USA have defeated hunger once and for all? It is because, as a human being, I too am just as capable of doing so. But despite been created in God's image and likeness like the Americans and the other people of the world, my people have constantly been ravaged by hunger and sometimes died of it. Our vast landscape of arable land is littered with bones of victims of hunger. Very often, I and my people have found ourselves eating food donated through humanitarian agencies by other people who happen to be at peace and more hardworking.

I know that we, South Sudanese people, are not lazy as such but have been held captive for long by a series of civil wars and degrading humiliation. But now we should wake up and till the land so that we defeat hunger and regain our lost dignity and stand shoulder to shoulder with other human beings.

Almost the entire South Sudan comprises arable land that can support agriculture. Credible research has found that ninety per cent (90%) of the land is suitable for agriculture. But the main agricultural land amounts to about fifty per cent (50%) of our national territory. Yet although the nation has over 30 million hectares of arable land, only five per cent (5%) is currently under cultivation.

It is the duty of all citizens and their governments at all levels to change this equation to ensure that at least 30 million hectares are fully utilised for the benefit of all. If we do this, there will be no talk of unemployment or hunger in our young nation.

Crop production and horticulture

Among the crops that do particularly well in South Sudan are sorghum, maize, rice, wheat, finger millet, cassava, groundnuts, beans, sesame, sunflower and sweet potatoes. The main fruit varieties include banana, mango, guava, lemon, orange, plantain, pineapple and papaya. Main vegetables include onion, okra, cabbage, eggplant, pumpkin and cucumber, coffee and tea. Other agricultural products include sugarcane and cotton. To date, however, people have been growing these things at subsistence level. But there are some compatriots who aim at expanding their farming so that they can be supplying the local markets.

If South Sudanese focus on serious farming, our country is endowed with enough agricultural land, and we will be totally self-sufficient so far as food is concerned. In fact, our nation has what it takes to become the breadbasket of Africa, if not the whole world. To demonstrate brotherly love, our national motto should be justice for all, freedom from hunger for all, equal access to food and prosperity for all and fear and love of God. This would make him continue to bless our young nation and her people.

Flock and livestock

Our unique domestic animals like cattle, sheep and goats, camels, mules, donkeys and pigs are our heritage and source of national pride. As I write, South Sudan has an estimated 11 million head of cattle. Livestock is an important source of livelihood to the two-thirds of the national population that live in the plains, semi-arid and pastoral areas.

In the past, meat was exported from South Sudan to the Middle East. The primary animal products included meat, leather and dairy. Unfortunately, as I write, South Sudan is a net importer of preserved milk. Our domestic animals have been ravaged by serious animal diseases that claim many of them every year. The upshot of herders competing over grazing land and water sources has often been animosity that has sometimes degenerated into fatal conflicts that even threaten national security.

It is the responsibility of each and every citizen and the local and national governments to come up with good, workable policies and strategies for the management of our livestock. The first thing should be to resolve the disputes involving our pastoral communities amicably by coming up with ways of sharing both grazing lands and water sources, particularly during dry seasons.

The second thing should be to look into ways of preventing or managing the rampant diseases that kill our people's animals in thousands each year.

The third step should be to encourage zero-grazing among the citizens, especially the herders, to avoid unnecessary quarrels or fights among them. Besides creating harmony between traditional herders and farmers, this will also encourage each and every citizen to do farming and keep some animals concurrently.

The fourth step should be to change the mind-set of the pastoralists and instil entrepreneurial spirit in them so that they start seeing the work they do as a business and start managing it as so. If our animals are well managed, South Sudan will be one of the world's leading suppliers of meat, other dairy products and leather. Let us not turn what God has blessed our nation with into a curse.

Poultry

In South Sudan, it is hard to find, especially in the countryside, a household without a good number of chickens. Let us assume that each household has 10 chickens on average, and there are 7 million households nationwide. This would translate into 70 million chickens.

Some families also keep other kinds of poultry that can be estimated to be in thousands if not hundreds of thousands nationally. By eating their eggs and meat, our people become healthier and those who keep the poultry earn income from selling them and their products. Unfortunately, our people have been depending on imported chicken and eggs from the neighbouring countries. This is because poultry has not yet reached a commercial stage in South Sudan.

Hence, it is the duty of our policy makers to encourage the keeping of poultry all over the country both for local consumption and export. This will also become a national and individual source of income and translate into jobs. I don't mean to encourage selfishness, but let us be determined to consume locally produced food, as this will be a way of building our nation.

Forestry

In the young Republic of South Sudan, forests make up twenty-nine per cent (29%) of the nation, and this translates into approximately 191,667 sq. km. Moreover, our woodlands yield high-grade timber that includes teak, mahogany and ebony, eucalyptus and pines, among others. The teak plantation is the most expansive of its kind in the world. In Central Equatoria, some teak plantations are in Kegulu, but the oldest forest reserves are Kawale, Lijo, Loka West and Nuni. In Western Equatoria, timber resources include mvuba trees at Zamoi.

The forests yield high quality oils like shea, and we also have a great potential in the production of Gum Arabic. Generally, these forests have a high biodiversity and are rich with flora and fauna. Ironically, we currently spend a lot of money to import timber from neighbouring countries like Uganda and Kenya for construction purposes. It boggles one's mind why our young nation should not speed up the exploitation of such resources! Unless circumstances demanded that we import things, we should not do it as this calls for spending our foreign currency. We should stop being consumers of foreign goods for the sake of it. There is nothing readymade anywhere; even natural water requires distillation to be fit for consumption. There is a tendency for people to admire and love what belong to others, as a result of which they sell theirs, sometimes even when it is superior, to buy what belongs to others.

Thus, it is the primary duty of our nation to make some well-thought-out plans on the exploitation of our hardwoods and execute them in the production of timber for both local and external consumption. We should exercise care, though, in doing the harvesting and replace the trees we cut down with others that we plant so that we do not endanger our environment by drastically reducing the forest cover. Our motto in forest conservation should be: Plant 5 trees for every tree cut. This is a reliable source of income and employment; so let us build with what we have locally before we go looking for wood next door!

Mineral Resources

South Sudan is richly blessed with huge deposits of unrefined gold, diamonds, limestone, iron ore, copper, chromium, zinc, tungsten, mica and silver, among other minerals. Bentiu has large deposit of oil, and Warrap, Lakes and Jonglei have good reserves, too. At the time of my writing, South Sudan largely depends on oil revenue, which contributes about ninety per cent (90%) of its national income. Exploration and exploitation of other resources is in progress.

It is worth mentioning that before South Sudan got her independence, Sudan entered into agreements with some foreign companies to exploit these natural resources, particularly the oil reserves. Needless to say, these agreements did not favour South Sudan. Although it was clearly spelled out in the Comprehensive Peace Agreement (CPA) that the money accruing from oil should be shared equally between North and South Sudan during the CPA period, the Sudan deceitfully took the lion's share of the oil revenues. Not only that, Sudan planned, and has not yet abandoned this plan, to hold on to some parts of South Sudan such as Abyei that are rich in oil. That is why the status of Abyei and the boundary between the two nations remained unclear before the end of the CPA, although they were specifically stipulated in the CPA and were to have been clarified prior to the South Sudan Referendum. This is the biggest national and regional problem.

Another potential problem that South Sudan inherited

upon becoming independent is that of the oil agreements that had been entered into between Sudan and foreign companies. Some of these companies still operate inside the South Sudan territory. Although it may not be happy now with some of them, it will take longer time for South Sudan to come up with a strategy of freeing herself from these agreements and establishing new, favourable agreements with people of her own choice. These companies, particularly the ones operating in the disputed areas, are nagged by not knowing where to pay allegiance, whether to Sudan or South Sudan. This is because they can't tell in advance as to which part of the border their oil fields will fall at the conclusion of the Abyei Protocol and when the border will be determined between the two nations. And, of course, Jesus Christ said that it is difficult for one to equally and honestly serve two masters, for he will either despises one master and honour the other. So now we can't tell with certainty where they are leaning; unfortunately, some of them may end up being a part of the oil problem between the two countries rather than a solution. Let me categorize this conflict of allegiance as number two among the major problems. And I see it continuing until the conclusion of the Abyei Protocol as well as when the acceptable border of the two countries will be determined.

But probably, the worst of nation's problems is that of greed for oil money among some of our influential politicians and other opinion leaders. You see, some of these leaders lobbied, agreed and signed illicit accords to do with oil explorations and extractions in certain parts of South Sudan with certain individuals and agencies right before and after CPA. And even today, similar deals are going on secretly involving oil and other minerals.

In view of this, the right questions that a nationalistic,

sound-minded, loving person to ask are: Who owns the national resources? Are they individually, regionally or nationally owned? Who has the right to enter into or terminate such agreements? Do our poor people really know the complexity and implication of legally binding international pacts? Some of those agreements bind the nation for long or are irrevocable once signed. To me, this is the third major problem which needs urgent, national attention or else we will end up, unknowingly or knowingly, not only selling the mineral resources but also the whole nation. It is better for one to have little but live and die with dignity than to have everything and live and die in shame.

According to me, if we really stick to our six national moral principles or core values of justice for all, liberty for all, prosperity for all, equality for all, and also if we really fear and love God and love each other as we actually love ourselves, our oil and other mineral resources will make all of us plus our own nation of South Sudan richer than any other rich nations of the world. But if we fight over them, the big regional and international vampires will jump in, support the ignorant and the selfish to fight among themselves as they plunder our natural resources, then go away and leave this blessed land poor and in total confusion like many other looted countries that we see in the world.

Of course, those of our countrymen who are greedy would not mind that as it will present an opportunity to side with outsiders and partake in the looting of their own wealth at the expense of the poor majority. Then they would run way and invest this bloody money in foreign lands. Or they may opt to remain inside South Sudan, arm and protect themselves and their ill-gotten gains and become the shining stars in the midst of paupers. But these people would not enjoy life despite their riches because their conscience would be constantly pricking them. They would live in fear, afraid of themselves and their own people.

Of course, I am not denying the fact that people are created and gifted differently, as a result of which some are better placed to acquire wealth than others even if they are placed in the same environments and given equal opportunities. In such cases, there is no problem if one honestly sweats and gets richer to the level of earning the title: "millionaire", for "He who gathers money little by little makes it grow" (Prov13:11b). Wealth that is earned honestly benefits its owners and becomes a blessing to other human beings, and the children of the owners of the wealth can inherit it honourably and pass it on to their descendants. This is in line with God's word to Adam: "By the sweat of your brow you will eat your food" (Gen.3:19a).

But that is not so with ill-gotten wealth, one that is acquired through a series of dishonest deals that involve knowingly violating and trampling other people's rights in the process of acquiring it. This type of wealth is short-lived and can even kill prematurely. Short-cut to riches always result in regrettable curses and lasting pain. Concerning people who pursue them the Bible says:

> People who want to get rich fall into temptation
> and a trap and into many foolish and harmful
> desires that plunge men into ruin and destruction.
> For the love of money is a root of all kinds
> of evil. Some people, eager for money, have
> wandered from the faith and pierced themselves
> with many griefs (1Tim.6:9-10).

Our people should not be in a hurry to acquire riches by

resorting to fraudulent deals because "dishonest money dwindles away" (Prov13:11a). Instead, let us seek to follow the right way to acquire wealth so that God blesses and enables us to enjoy it and in the end pass it over to our children's children to also enjoy it and in turn pass it to their children.

In order for all of us to benefit from our God-given mineral resources instead of allowing them to become national curse, it is incumbent upon all of us and our governments at various levels to craft new policies or improve on the existing ones that govern mining. These rules and policies should be guided by our moral principles of justice for all, liberty for all, prosperity for all and equality for all. The fear and love of God and the love for one another should be the glue that keeps our people together us they enjoy their wealth. The moment these vital resources are put into proper use, there will be big job opportunities both for the South Sudanese people and their foreign expatriates. If we eat lovingly together, we will laugh or cry together and live and work together for our common welfare.

Tourism

There are about 7 national parks which include Boma, Nimule National, South National, Bandingalo National and Sudd Wetland National Parks. There are also 12 game reserves in South Sudan, among which is Zeraf Wildlife Reserve. These parks and reserves have varieties of wildlife animals that include kob antelopes, hartebeests, bongo and topis, giant and red river hogs, elephants, buffalos, giraffes, chimpanzees and forest monkeys, hippos, hyenas, gazelles, zebras, ostriches, leopards and lions, among others. Nimule National Park also contains Mount Kei Forest Reserve and Mount Otzi Forest Reserve. Protection of flora and fauna is a national policy.

These national parks and game reserves offer national and international tourists an opportunity to watch diverse of wildlife species. At the time of my writing, there are several hotels and lodges operating in those tourist sites in South Sudan.

Tourism is one of the major sources of individual and national incomes in many parts of the world. Similarly, if our tourism sector is protected and managed well, it will greatly benefit our nation and her citizens in terms of employment and financial income. These are some of the direct benefits, although indirect benefits are equally huge. These include enhancing our regional and national influence and attracting foreign investors.

But as a way of promoting our tourism to national, regional and international tourists, South Sudanese people and their governments at various levels must first address the following major issues.

First, we must deal with insecurity at the local and national level. If we really want to build our tourism sector, we must love our tourists as ourselves to the extent of making them feel at home in our country. Let them move around and sleep anywhere peacefully.

Second, animal poaching could benefit individuals but not all of us. If we give local poachers a free rein, regional and international poachers will join them and destroy our beautiful wildlife heritage. Thus, it is important that our government stamps out unregulated poaching.

Third, it is the moral duty of all those dealing with wildlife conservations and tourism to, first of all, instil proper discipline in the minds and hearts of their personnel so that they respect, uphold and enforce all ethical norms governing these vital national sectors. This is because conventional wisdom requires that we practise what we preach.

Customs and Immigrations

In any part of the world, customs and immigration are huge income earners for any government and its citizens. They are significant sources of employment in any nation.

South Sudan has six borders with its neighbouring countries—Sudan, Central Africa Republic (CAR), the Democratic Republic of the Congo (DRC), Uganda, Kenya and Ethiopia. There is a lot of trafficking between Kenya, Uganda, Sudan and DRC. And, needless to say, the more the volume of traffic, the more money collected by the government daily. The money is in the form of custom duty and immigration charges.

As I pen this part of the book, Juba International Airport is the main link connecting South Sudan and the outside world. Besides, all the ten cities in our ten states have national airports. It is common practice for the nation to be paid by the users of the airports. The other income emanates from the issuing of visas and customs fees.

If this money is duly collected and put to use in line with our national principles of justice for all, liberty for all, prosperity for all, equality for all, and backed up with our fear and love for God and love for each other, it would greatly benefit our nation.

However, it is in these departments that corruption is most prevalent. And if such a vice is left to thrive, it will lead to a national security problem. This is because the thick blanket of corruption will blindfold the national guards and make them to allow the unallowable to come in and terrorise us within our nation.

In my life, I have been to quite a few places in the world. For instance, I have visited and stayed in Kenya many times during my college studies and during other occasions. I have been to Ethiopia and Thailand once. I have visited USA several times, transiting through London, Uganda, Dubai, Amsterdam and Qatar. And during this time, I was subjected to very strict customs and immigration procedures. Some of those nations do not allow passengers from unfriendly nations to pass through their airports without the requisite exit visas. It is imperative that you obtain the exit visa from the relevant embassy at the port or place of origin before you board the plane, else the relevant airline will not allow you into the plane.

Although I have been a frequent visitor to the States and have friends there, whenever I go there I contend with the same strict customs and immigration requirements. Nor does my being a pastor exempt me from having my papers scrutinized or from physical screening. This is because it is one thing to don the priestly garb and another thing to live out what is expected of priests. Priesthood has been given a bad name by some unfaithful elements in the world, seeking to use the trust that goes with the name to achieve their dirty goals. Hence, there is nothing wrong with subjecting pastors to the same checks like any other human being.

I personally enjoy the way the customs and immigration personnel painstakingly execute their day-to-day tasks in those countries. Not that they are mean and unfriendly to clients; rather, they do what they do to protect their nationals and others on their soil.

Many of my South Sudanese compatriots have been outside our national borders more than I and might have learned better than I how other people manage their customs and immigration work. But the question is whether we put into practice those learned lessons to benefit our young nation. To me, customs and immigration rules and regulations are a necessary part of our nation and the general welfare of any nation below the sun.

Therefore, any customs and immigration workers must be people who exhibit the spirit of nationalism, people who put their national interests above their own personal aspirations. Although jobs in these important sectors are highly paying, they are too important to be given to citizens who are merely driven by the reward of job. If that happens, we will strangle our nation alive and bury it in the deepest grave of selfishness and financial greed.

Taxation

In any part of the world, the citizens are what comprised a nation. A government is a structured tool that people use to attain their collective goals. But since it is impersonal, its people choose some of their members to operate it for the common good of all. Without people, there is no government, and that is why the former USA President Abraham Lincoln referred to it as "Government of the people, for the people, by the people". A government is made by the people themselves; it is managed and operated by the people themselves, and its acquired benefits are for the people themselves.

If our people get to understand that people own, manage and operate their own government but through the principle of delegation whereby people select among themselves some of their capable members to run it, then they would understand that they have the unavoidable duty to support it morally, spiritually and materially for their own common well-being. That way they would see the reason behind protecting it even by shedding their own blood in the event of local and external aggression.

Another way in which people support their government is through what is known as personal income tax. In this case, every citizen above 18 years of age is required by law to contribute to his government a certain minimal percentage of his personal income. One's income could be in the form of personal assets like buildings, vehicles, pieces of land, monthly salary, donations, livestock and flock of sheep and goat, profit accruing from business activities, just to mention a few. For example, if my salary income per month is SSP2, 000 and our government national taxation policy stipulates that people within this range of income pay fifteen per cent (15%) as tax, then I am obligated to remit monthly SSP300 to a specified government bank account and keep my bank slips as proof that I have fulfilled this statutory duty. I am supposed to do likewise in respect of any other source of income that I make, whether daily, monthly or annually.

Taxes are paid daily, monthly or annually, depending on the type of income as well as the policy governing taxation system. Tax evasion has severe repercussions in any nation, since everyone is legally obligated to support their own government.

Another way in which the government gets money daily, not only from its nationals but also from foreigners, is through Value Added Tax (VAT) that is legally levied on any items purchased. VAT is added on anything bought in a shop, factory, hotel, etc. if it is Vat-able. For example, if I buy a car costing SSP203,500 before VAT and such commodities attract 16%VAT, then I am obligated to pay SSP32,560 (16/100 X 203,500) on top of SSP203,500. But though I will pay the seller a total of SSP236,060, he will transmit SSP32, 560 to the government. Yet collecting of VAT on behalf of the government does not exempt such a business person from paying taxes emanating from his income. Other things that are charged VAT include air tickets and bus tickets.

The volume of business transactions that take place in our nation of South Sudan daily is huge. Accordingly, our government would get a lot of income daily from VAT if this tax were to be collected as it should, especially if the system of collecting this money is computerised. Yet if the work is not done well, what would have brought income will turn out to be a fertile ground for corruption to thrive.

The primary supports that people get from their own government include security, infrastructure like road network, health and educational services, etc. But how does the government finance these national programmes? Taxation is one of the reliable sources of revenue through which the government funds these vital services to its citizens. With this awareness, why would people be unwilling to generously pay taxes to their government?

I don't have all the answers as to why people are reluctant to pay taxes to their own government, but experience has shown three main reasons behind their refusal to pay taxes. The first one is their ignorance about their government's taxation policies and regulations as well as the importance of paying taxes. The second reason is failure on the government to provide the promised services. If people don't get services from the government, then their enthusiasm for paying taxes wanes. Third, if their taxes are not handled accountably and transparently and instead end up in individual pockets, people will try by all means to evade taxation.

What then should be done to make our people pay their

taxes faithfully and without needing to be pressured? I believe if we and our government can effectively address the above three and other secondary issues, taxation will become a pleasant national duty to all. Let us support our government, not individuals, with our taxes so that the government can in turn support us.

Games and Sports

South Sudan is known for traditional and modern sports. Among the traditional ones are wrestling, mock and tug of war. Modern sports include football, basketball, tennis, rugby and athletics, just to name a few.

If these games and sports are purposely organised and supported by the government at all levels, they will make us known and enhance our image as a nation in the global community. They could also become sources of individual and national income and create job opportunities.

Art and Music

Modern music like hip-hop, reggae and other Western genres of music are now popular in South Sudan. Artistically, South Sudan has experts in fine art; for example, there are those who draw on canvas, cartoonists, etc.

As a result, plans should be carried out by those concerned and our local and national governments towards the promotion of these potentially profitable sectors. People who are engaged in music and art need government support to build their morale and material support to encourage them to be innovative and hard-working for the common good of our nation. With the necessary support that they require, the creativity of these people will explode and make art and music reliable sources of individual and national income as well as a means of providing employment.

Foreign Aid

As a newly independent nation, South Sudan has received and will continue to receive different forms of assistance from friendly nations, aid agencies and individuals in and outside Africa. These humanitarian and development support includes cash, equipment, furniture and skilled people to help us expertise in different areas. Some of this is short-term assistance, but some of it is long-term aid.

Aid, in whatever form, is meant for projects that are supposed to help people nationally or locally. For example, there is some kind of assistance that is meant for building of government capacity to enable it stand on its own feet in delivering needed social, economic and political services to its people. Such aid comes directly or indirectly to the government, and it is disbursed in various forms like equipment and tools, furniture and hard cash. But there is also help from donors that comes through international non-governmental organizations (NGOs) and national agencies to fund some humanitarian and development programmes, both to the South Sudanese returnees and host communities.

If this foreign support is received and implemented in a transparent and accountable manner, it will benefit people in the entire nation of South Sudan and their own government. And upon seeing the positive impact it has both on the government and its people, foreign donors will continue to pour in more help for the well-being of our nation. This is a vital area which could easily enhance individual and national incomes; it has potential for job creation.

But the moment the rules and policies guiding external aid are deliberately violated by NGOs and individual South Sudanese to suit their personal interests, the support will immediately cease. This will result in dire consequences upon our people. For example, the image of our nation will be tarnished, services that were supported by foreign assistances discontinued, our nation will be denied foreign aid in future, and the dignity of the persons concerned with the aid will be negatively impacted. Legal action may be taken against such people.

Needless to say, aid disbursed in an environment that lacks structures that will facilitate accountability risks being squandered by corrupt people. Therefore, it is imperative that all South Sudanese people and their government come up with strict policies for channelling foreign assistance to the areas it is intended so that it results in improving the welfare of all.

Debt, in whatever form, comes with some strings attached. The worst of these strings is the lender deliberately meddling in the personal affairs of the debtor. Debt also destroys the personal dignity of the debtor while boosting the ego of the lender. As the Bible says, "The rich rule over the poor, and the borrower is a servant to the lender" (Prov. 22:7). An interesting aspect of debt is the way it accumulates progressively a bit by bit and through accruing interest until it becomes a formidable mountain.

Although our nation currently faces some critical issues that urgently require huge amount of funds to address them, it would be prudent to slow the rate of borrowing so that we do not reach a point where we cannot honour our commitments or where we have mortgaged our future generations. When we must borrow, the deal should be a well-thought-out one to ensure that its repayment terms are affordable. Observing this is what will enable us to live now and in future as a dignified, debt-free nation whose people move with their heads high in the community of world nations. As individuals and even as a nation, let us learn to be satisfied with what we have in our hands more than what belongs to someone else.

Summary

If South Sudan and her people exercise self-control where making riches is concerned, craft policies to keep in check unplanned national development and instead come up with some SMART (Specific, Measurable, Achievable, Realistic, Time-bound) national policies, plans and regulations, our nation will have a formidable national foundation on which to grow. Justice for all, liberty for all, prosperity for all and equality for all should be the moral national principles, the pillars that uphold our national foundation. Fear and love of God and love for one another should be the reliable, long-lasting binding ligaments that bind our people together.

With this spirit of brotherhood, we will be able to utilise our arable land, water resources, agricultural benefits, mineral resources, income from tourism, customs and immigration, tax, games and sports, art and music and foreign aid for our common welfare. As a result, our nation will soon become one of the strongest and prosperous nations. Our vast resources will indeed be a blessing from above.

But if we hate one another and selfishly try to enjoy our lives individually by ripping of our nation, we will tear ourselves and our nation apart for the joy of our enemies. Then we will live a shameful life that is full of regrets, hatred and poverty. Instead of benefiting us, our vast resources will become a curse.

It is our collective responsibility, we and our people's government, to uphold and protect our moral national principles and to honestly mobilise and use our huge national resources to build a durable national foundation on which the young Republic of South Sudan stands firmly as it moves confidently and briskly along the rough road of development. Let us stop, once and for all, childish blame games, since in the eyes of God and fellow human beings we are collectively responsible for our good deeds as well as our mistakes. No one can make our young republic into a great nation on our behalf, for as the late Abraham Lincoln said, "You cannot escape the responsibility of tomorrow by evading it today." The choice of remaining with a struggling nation and forging a respectable republic is ours!

Chapter Three

THE WAR ON THE SYSTEMS AND THE LOST NATIONAL FUNDS, THE WAR ON ILLITERACY AND LANGUAGE PROBLEM

Introduction

Who is to blame, the poor government systems that allow the thief to steal or the thief who steals because the government has not come up with proper and enforceable measures to prevent stealing? As I seek to tackle this contentious issue of alleged national financial scandal, you will agree with me that it is better, if possible, to catch a thief and punish him. But the problem is: what do you do if you can't catch the thief so as to discipline him, or, even worse, the number of thieves is too large, or the thieves are too powerful?

Personally, I blame, first of all, the poor government systems that allowed the thieves to access and loot our national resources. I suggest the following be done to deter people with evil intentions from plundering our wealth, although this is not all that can be done: the people's government should urgently improve on the government systems so as to prevent further theft. And since the people involved in the scandal seem to be many and powerful, and also since the bulk of the alleged money is said to be stashed in accounts outside the country, I suggest our young government forgive but ask them to voluntarily return these funds and invest them in South Sudan to boost our national economy.

Needless to say, if this issue is not handled with a high level of integrity and maturity, it may terribly backfire and polarize our people. Forgiving one another is Biblical and powerful way of solving seemingly intractable problems under the sun. Seeking good national systems should take precedence over running after the lost national resources.

Another big issue that I discuss in this chapter has to do with the high rate of illiteracy in our nation and lack of a national language that is understood by all. My own research has established that both Arabic and English are used only in the urban areas. The effect of this has been dividing our citizens rather than uniting them. Hence, the search for a unifying language should be given priority. High illiteracy among our people is also a major national issue that deserves immediate solution. If this issue is effectively addressed, our people will get to know and protect their rights and become employable. Literacy will also promote national unity and peaceful co-existence. In the following pages, follow me as I discuss some possible approaches in creating government systems and recovering plundered national funds.

The War on the Systems and the Lost National Funds

First and foremost, I really don't know how much of our young nation's money has gone into individual hands, if at all any money has been lost. This is because I am not in a position to ascertain this. Yet I am entitled to know because of the damage this has to our national image, especially in the eyes of the outsiders. The primary reason why I include this topic in this book is because financial scandals have become a nasty local and global issue these days and if not tackled well, may derail our country and destroy its moral fabric. Yet this issue requires a lot of wisdom to deal with. Actually in discussing it here, I do not mean to take sides when it comes to the scandal itself; rather, I intend to create awareness of its existence and its possible implications.

During and after the just-ended twenty-one-year civil war, I steadfastly maintained that the war on creating credible systems in South Sudan will be a difficult one; it would take longer time than the war of independence. What has transpired so far has not proven me wrong! I have a lot of good reasons in support of my assertion, but I will highlight only two of them here.

Since the beginning of our long national history (dating back to the nineteenth century) that was characterized by oppression and exploitation of man by man, the people of South Sudan have never had a chance to manage their affairs as a nation. Even when a few people from South Sudan were allowed to participate in the Khartoum Government around the twentieth century, they were not given managerial positions that would have enabled them to learn the skills and techniques of leadership and management. It is only briefly between 1972 and 1983 that a small percentage of the entire population of South Sudan attempted to learn on-the-job the ethics of management. But the actual machinery of leadership and management that drove the nation remained firmly in the hands of those in charge of the Khartoum Government. As a result, there were no actual systems of governance in South Sudan.

Then from 1983 to 2005, and especially in the lead up to 2011, the very few learned South Sudanese together with their entire population of their illiterate brothers and sisters got themselves deeply involved in a very nasty war of freeing their nation from oppression. During that time, we lost over 2 million people, both the literate and the illiterate alike, since the sword never discriminated. And even out of those who remained, a large number of the people were maimed to spend the rest of their days hobbling with the help of crutches. Other undesirable results of the war include a big number of orphans, widows, widowers and people who were affected psychologically. During the war, many unlucky youngsters grew up and died without an education. An equally large number of those who are alive is still illiterate.

In the bush people learned how to use weapons of war—not good governance! According to my own understanding, the people of South Sudan did not go to their countryside to learn good management and leadership skills; they went there to fight to free themselves and obtain what they lacked.

We shouldn't deny the fact that truth is always bitter, but it is worth saying, anyway. During the long period of our struggle, and even after the official declaration of the independence of South Sudan in 2011, some of our brothers and sisters in Sudan have been telling us the bitter truth, albeit scornfully, "Southerners don't know how to manage themselves." To me, those are honest words, for they are aware that their forefathers and they themselves have ensured that we remain behind in the darkest shadow of ignorance so far as leadership and management are concerned. Their unfriendly, inhumane plan that was characterized by oppression and exploitation was the major cause of the splitting up of Sudan.

Let us ask sincere questions and accept objective answers. How long did it take for other nations of the world to be where they are in terms of efficiency and effectiveness so far as systems of good governance are concerned? And how much effort are they still putting to keep improving on those systems? It virtually took hundreds of years, if not thousands, to reach where they are. They have written and are still writing relevant books, policy documents, periodic magazines and articles, and they are making endless researches and documenting their findings in an effort to improve their systems of government. But despite all these good systems of governance, terrible mistakes have been made and are still being made on a daily basis.

Now as we discuss this scandal, how old is the Republic of South Sudan? Your answer is as good as mine. I don't normally judge other people's opinion. Some people suppose that the systems of the government of South Sudan should have matured by the day of independence and become more or less like the ones of the developed and developing countries. Such people imagine that our national leaders, who have endured unspeakable brutality during a series of civil wars, should be like other world leaders who were born and brought up in enabling socio-economic, political and cultural environments. Of course, people are entitled to their opinion since we are living in a fairly democratic world today. I also agree that my arguments do not justify malpractices on a personal or national level. But please move with me to the next level of my thinking.

Of course, man, including you and I, is a thief by nature, right from the Garden of Eden when he stole God's fruit of the forbidden tree. This innate spirit of theft makes him to take any possible advantage and loopholes, with the aim of fulfilling his selfish interests. It is this depraved behaviour of humans that compelled God to include this article to the Ten Commandments: "You shall not steal" (Deut.5:19).

When given a chance to freely decide and apply their will, people will individually and collectively rob and loot anything under the sun. People steal ideas; they steal money and steal other vital resources. As if that is not enough, they even steal and enslave fellow human beings. Because of this spirit of deceit and theft in the heart of man, some of the best world looters believe that "to cheat a fool is not a sin." Indeed, we still have many fool cheaters in our world, although they fail to recognize that cheating is itself a sin in the eyes of God and moral being.

At very, very high level, individuals, agencies and nations still cheat and steal from each other ideas and engage in illegal trade deals particularly when it comes to borrowing and lending. This sometimes leads to countries, especially Third World countries, getting saddled with huge debts that they cannot service but keep hoping that they will finally be cancelled.

Actually, if the just God were to declare judgement on all of us, individually and collectively, because of any kind of theft we have been involved in, all of us would be victims.

If national resources have been lost as alleged, how did it happen, and who is to blame? Are we still losing money belonging to the national treasury or has the trend stopped? What is the way forward so far as addressing this national crime is concerned? In the remaining section, I will try to answer questions relating to this complex topic.

How did theft of the funds occur, and who is to blame? I don't know how it occurred because I was not involved, and even today I am still not involved. In fact, I don't waste time and energy on blame games whenever a problem occurs; instead, I take mistakes seriously as a good lesson so that I don't repeat them. I prefer going for the solution to the problem.

In this case, I feel blame should be directed to the poor government systems. If proper systems with checks and balances and backed by enforceable laws were in place, there would have been no talks of the unfortunate loss of national funds. Good systems would have prevented the loss and ensure good governance. But if there were and still are systems in place but the people decided to violate them, then there seems to be cartels somewhere to facilitate illegal deals.

But who was or is still supposed to put in place and enforce the correct government systems? The people's government, consisting of the executive, the legislature and the judiciary, has the sole authority to execute this vital national task on behalf of its citizens. It is not a one-man job; it is a collective venture, involving all three arms of the government and all government officials.

Now who took the people's resources and how many are they? Did some foreigners partake in this unhealthy exercise? I believe the omniscient and omnipresent God and those in question are the ones to give us the right answers.

Whenever people talk of financial scandal either in the government or private sector in any part of the world, it is always at a very minimal scale, concerning just one person or a few people. But what makes ours quite unusual is the way it seems to involve almost all the government employees and other national citizens. For me, it appears as it was not deliberately planned and executed by those concerned.

Please allow me to paint a mental picture by comparing the alleged huge and uncontrollable theft of national resources to a sea of moral corruption and the weak government systems to a weak dam of moral goodness. It looks like the big sea of moral corruption suddenly busted its bank, rapidly descended downhill and demolished the weak dam of moral goodness. Unfortunately, the dirty waters of the sea surged and sprayed over almost all the people in the government plus their closest national onlookers. It is as if our people had been denied some vital necessities of life during the long period that they were struggling for independence and now want to make up for the lost time by chasing wealth. No human being seems to be able to resist the force of the surging "dirty wave" if he happens to be around. Indeed, even those of our national figures whom we looked up to in the past because of their admirable ethical values are now alleged to have taken part in this national financial scandal.

Ultimately, the weak government systems are to blame because it is as if the national resources started coming in before proper government systems that could ensure ethical transparency and moral accountability were firmly put in place. These government systems include proper, strict banking systems; strict financial policies and regulations implemented by financial experts in all branches of government and relevant agencies; effective, fair and professionally run anti-corruption agency; impartial national law that is interpreted and enforced by professionals; impartial judiciary systems; standardised stationery for financial accountability that is easy for use, etc. The list is long.

Were the funds lost only in the past, or we are still losing them? Personally, I don't know what is happening because I am not privy to what happens in the relevant departments. But if my analogy of a strong sea of ethical corruption overrunning a weak moral dam of goodness is anything to go by, then the loss of national funds is still on-going, and it will not stop unless a strong, reliable moral dam is put in place to stop the strong and rapid flow of the dirty waters from the sea of moral corruption.

I am personally afraid of and totally disagree with those who loudly speak about this financial scandal. Because I am fully persuaded that without putting a proper, executable moral dam of transparency and accountability in place, these funds even if faithfully returned by the "Good Zacchaeus", will still swiftly go out with the dirty waters of the moral sea of corruption or find their way into other big pockets.

Thus, what is the way forward when it comes to dealing with this national issue? First of all, we should understand that the major issue facing the young nation of South Sudan is not the loss of public funds but the weak systems that made it possible for individuals to access and take the money away with impunity. Loss of money is a mere symptom of the underlying cause, and if this root cause is not completely addressed, more funds and other national resources will continue going into private hands at the expense of the general public.

As a result, for good governance's sake, we should urgently and intentionally use local and external machinery to build inviolable and reliable national systems and enforce them impartially, mercilessly and honestly. In crafting these government systems, we should be guided by our national principles of justice for all, liberty for all, prosperity for all, equality for all, fear and love of God as well as love for each other.

The other thing to do in dealing with this national issue is to preach the importance of God's love and love of fellow human beings as a way of appealing to people to mind the future of this nation. Financial scandals, albeit of minimal scale, have torn and are still tearing some nations apart because of being casually handled by disrespectfully humiliating those involved. Of course, if they are treated as if they are the only bad people on earth, they will retreat to their cocoons of self-protection, doing all they can to justify their behaviour and, if possible, hitting back mercilessly on their accusers. That is why we should draw upon the wisdom of our native saying, "Dɔm rueny ku tit rɔt," "Protect yourself as you catch the thief."

This warning shows the difficulty of catching just one thief. Hence, even if you are a government, backed by a formidable force and a justice system and soldiers, what do you honestly think will happen when you go after a big number of well-organised thieves? The situation is compounded if those who are supposed to catch the thief and enforce the law are also among those involved in the theft. You can be sure that there will be a nasty, bloody fight. Instead of engaging in this impossible war, why not fight for the proper establishment of government systems that are sure to arrest the unfortunate trend of stealing national resources?

Sometimes a grave moral problem needs simple wisdom to address peacefully. Let's see here how the Son of God addresses a controversial, life threatening moral problem. One day the teachers of the Law and the Pharisees took a woman caught in adultery to Jesus Christ and sought his opinion about the case, reminding him according to the Mosaic law, her kind of sin was punishable by death through stoning. Aware of their ill-intention, Jesus told them: 'If anyone of you is without sin, let him be the first to throw a stone at her' (Jn.8:7b). "At this, those who heard began to go away one at a time, the older ones first…" (vs.9a). Then Jesus said, 'Woman, where are they? Has no one condemned you?' 'No one sir', she said." 'Then neither do I condemn you,' Jesus declared. Go now and leave your life of sin' (vs.10-11).

As you can see, all that Jesus did was to make them aware that they were sinful people, too. The ensuing conviction deterred them from stoning her, and they started departing one by one, leaving the nervous culprit standing before the holy Judge and thinking that he was going to condemn her. But Jesus Christ knows that meeting wrong with wrong is never the solution to any problem. So he warned her against sin and set her free.

I strongly believe that if Jesus Christ were to ask those South Sudanese people who have not stolen and other concerned foreigners to pick and throw stones at those accused of financial scandal, people will speed off together as they flee from the Lord and leave the offenders standing nervously before him. As a result, he will forgive them and tell them to abandon their sinful ways.

Now, as none of us is truly sinless, the best we can do is simply admonish and forgive our brothers and sisters for the sake of our national unity and peaceful co-existence! The cohesiveness of our society is far more important than any amount of lost funds. Let the spirit of forgiveness and tolerance be one of the ingredients that bind us together and sustain our self-esteem as a people.

The third and the last step in the quest about better safeguards of our national resources is to ask ourselves, where are the alleged missing funds, and who is benefiting from them? If the funds were smuggled out and banked or invested in foreign countries or just put in boxes and stored away in houses to rot and decay, this is wrong. It is even worse than the theft itself because we badly need them to invigorate our economy. You see when I move around Juba and other places inside South Sudan, I feel good seeing buildings coming up and new business enterprises. If these funds are invested locally, there will be more business activities and the attendant job creation.

If the owners of these funds are given freedom to use them locally, perhaps the Lord might convict them to act in love like Zacchaeus of the Bible and share them with the rest of us. Look here: "But Zacchaeus stood and said to the Lord, 'Look, Lord! Here and now I give half of my possessions to the poor, and if I have cheated anybody out of anything, I will pay back four times the amount'" (Lk.19:8). Zacchaeus was not forced to repent or share his wealth with others or refund for his ill-gotten gains; he voluntarily did it as good gesture and in response to personal conviction.

As to whether the conscience of the suspected people is troubling them, let's consider the wisdom of the late Abraham Lincoln, one of the greatest American Presidents. He said, "My great concern is not whether you have failed, but whether you are content with your failure." Like Abraham Lincoln, my major concern is not so much the lost funds but whether those who stole them are happy with their ethical failure. My deep concern is also due to the fact that we still do not seem to view effective government systems as a priority!

It is wise to forgive our brothers and sisters who might have taken the people's funds and appeal to them to return, bank and invest them locally to benefit fellow South Sudanese as well. That way God will forgive and bless them and the whole nation as well. We and our people's government must wage a continuous war when it comes to setting up national systems. We should never allow ourselves to be distracted by minor issues from our steadfastness. In dealing with the problems of our nation, we should learn to major on majors, not minors.

The War on Illiteracy and Language Problem

The long period of the South Sudan people's struggles had the negative effect of creating a big section of illiterate citizens against a few literate citizens. Furthermore, this young nation is very much fragmented in terms of the vernacular languages. There are 64 languages and dialects. These indigenous people are yet to come up with one particular language that can be used as a unifying medium of communication in the nation.

When our nation was a part of united Sudan, the official language of South Sudan was supposed to be Arabic, as this was the official national language. But a succession of Khartoum governments failed to promote this language aggressively, whether in the north or in other parts of the country. But the primary reason why almost all the people in the northern parts of Sudan know the language is simply because most of them are Muslims and the Koran is written and taught by it. For you to recite and understand verses in the Koran, you need to know at least basic Arabic. Being a first language and religious and business language to many, Arabic is a unifying national language in Sudan. It is spoken and used for written communication by all the Sudanese nationals. English, language of those who had colonized us initially and one of the most widely spoken languages in the world, is also used in Sudan, especially in the urban centres, albeit on a limited scale.

But in the case of South Sudan, the language situation is quite different and difficult. First, some people profess Christianity, while others believe in the ATRs (African traditional religions). Yet there are a few Muslims. There was and still is no great language attachment to their various religious beliefs. Even some of the South Sudanese illiterate Muslims now verbally speak Arabic. People are very much content with their unique mother tongues. Yet most of the natives prefer to communicate in their languages but do not see any benefits in learning to write them.

Arabic became the lingua franca in the urban areas in South Sudan because of being the language of business and language of instruction in schools in Sudan. English, on the other hand, was first used in South Sudan by colonialists and foreign missionaries. Indeed, the few people who turned to Christianity at the time were not compelled to learn English. Also it did not become a language of business since there were no trade that necessitated the use of English. As a result, it ended up as an urban language, used in schools, churches and government offices but still on a very limited level. The upshot was a host of local languages, Arabic and English being used in urban centres in South Sudan. Nonetheless, English and Arabic are the ones frequently used, with Arabic language being more commonly used because it is also the commercial language.

So far as language is concerned, our people became jacks of all trade but master of none. Now it is funny and easy to find a person using a little bit of English and Arabic plus his mother tongue, a mixture of three languages, while talking. Although people in South Sudan regard English to be their official language, the truth is that few know it.

Language problem plus illiteracy: if the government of South Sudan does not give the effort of coming up with an official language the important it deserves, lack of a unifying language will continue to be a major hindrance to development.

Let me share with you here some challenges associated with lack of a unifying language in our nation. First, although we so much need cohesion as a nation, our local languages have naturally divided us. With our indigenous people lacking a common mode of communication, they feel like strangers to one another, regarding at each other suspiciously. When circumstances bring them together, they don't understand each other unless there is someone to interpret. This language barrier does not permit them to learn from each other and work and live peacefully as citizens of the same nation. Although they may love each other, lack of a common language encourages them to confine themselves to their geographic localities where they can conduct their business with ease. This is the main cause of ethnic sentiment and the attendant lack of cohesion.

Worse still, in my opinion, the two foreign languages (English and Arabic) have further divided the people of South Sudan into two not very friendly groups. The first group is that of the elite that constitutes 24% of the general population. This comprises people who are viewed as favoured, who have jobs and live in urban centres. They communicate in either English or Arabic or both and regard farming as work for uneducated rural folks. The elite have good places to live in, whether owner-occupier or rented dwelling. Although they occasionally visit rural areas, the elite regard village life as primitive and hence, beneath them. When the elite talk with their rural folks, they use disparaging statements such as "You don't know anything; you are not educated", and so on and so forth. Unfortunately, some of them pretend they do not know their own mother tongues or look at their own vernacular as a primitive way of communication. Hence, they speak to their uneducated rural folks either in English or Arabic, even if they do not know these foreign languages. That is why some of us struggle to communicate in foreign languages they don't know well for fear that speaking through an interpreter will make them come across as less educated. These nauseating and similar acquired mannerisms end up alienating such people from their own illiterate villagers. Yet what they fail to realize is that we were complete human beings with valuable natural talents, wisdom, knowledge and understanding even before the advent of modern education. In other words, the superiority complex that the elite suffer from is misguided and misplaced.

What do you think should be the right response when your own brothers and sisters shun you, consider you primitive, uneducated and even lacking in natural intelligence? If you are not very careful, you may wrongly believe them, thinking that you are nothing, have nothing and can do nothing without them. You may even wrongly view them as gods.

We have been misusing foreign languages to destroy the image of the vast majority of our illiterate citizens by making them come across as primitive, despite their being talented in their own way. As a result, when their educated counterparts talk to them, they exhibit inferiority by timidly expressing their viewpoints. Indeed, it is not uncommon to hear them expressing inadequacy, saying, "We don't know anything because we are not educated; we have nothing; we are poor; we have no work"... the list goes on.

To appreciate the damage this does to their confidence, our rural folks still believe that they have no jobs even though they keep cattle and do farming, for they have been taught that a job is working in the office. The worst effect this mental abuse has had on our people, both the learned and the unlearned, is viewing their God-given languages as being inferior to foreign languages. In a nutshell, our rural, illiterate folks who make up about seventy-six per cent (76%) of our general population have been made to suffer low self-esteem by the way their educated counterparts treat them.

To me, foreign languages and a poor education system in South Sudan have not contributed to uniting our people but dividing the few urban elite and the vast rural illiterates. Worse still, the few urban citizens are divided, some seeing themselves as being pro Arabic and others pro English, depending on the language one knows better.

Sometimes the few educated people may inadvertently use language to exploit and oppress their illiterate folks. Unable to read and write even their own vernacular languages, these illiterate people do not understand their own national constitution, the laws of the land and other vital policy documents that govern them. Yet they are supposed to comply with such policies.

These illiterate people are also not aware of their human rights, much less how to defend them when violated. As a result, some of their unkind brothers and sisters have sometimes exploited this ignorance to rob them of their right resources.

Although our government and its agencies regularly carry out civic education to disseminate vital information to the public, I really doubt whether this has any significant impact. There are many ways by which illiterate people can be exploited and oppressed by fellow insensitive people.

Today's world is in a flux, and it requires people with some modern education to keep abreast of local and global affairs that are constantly changing. Those who don't know how to read and write are oftentimes behind news, unaware of what is happening around them and in other parts of the world. As a result, they are vulnerable to misinformation by those with ill or selfish motives. Illiterate people are always at the mercy of spin doctors who originate rumours and lies. Despite all that, illiterate people are always suspicious and sceptical of the elite. What do you think will happen if the majority didn't know how to read and write? Yet in South Sudan, that is where we are now as a nation.

What is the best way forward? It is common knowledge that identification of any problem is the beginning of its solution. But the worst thing that I have experienced is the manner in which people spend a lot of resources to establish the cause of a problem, only to praise their efforts and then file away their findings without taking any action to actualize the solution. I have also learned that although people are aware of their flaws, they often comfortably live with them without seeking solutions to them, perhaps hoping their weaknesses will one day vanish in the thin air. But let me assure you, unless you sweep your room, the dust will remain there.

Now if my compatriots and our government agree with me that the high illiteracy rate and lack of a well-developed lingua franca are priority national issues, and if we also mustered a strong will to address these issues amicably, we will find solutions to them within a very short period of time. Some of the simplest ways of addressing these national issues are suggested here below.

First, let's collectively identify one language, be it Arabic, English (as it is now the case), Bari, Nuer, etc., as the national language of communication.

Second, let's urgently mobilise and manage well the required resources.

Third, let our government officially embark on a campaign to give at least certain minimum education to all males and females, young and old, the disabled and the healthy in an effort to create a common language of communication. This project should be guided by a duly constituted committee of experts who will also give oversight to ensure it is implemented properly. The importance of the project justifies its progress being monitored, objectively evaluated and progress reports made to the commission of experts. Also decisions made by this commission should be enforceable in courts of law.

In the course of doing this, we will be solving the issue of high illiteracy. In addition, we are to develop our indigenous languages as part of our national heritage. This is because if they are well-developed, our people will cherish them and desire to use them even for general communication and record-keeping, especially if they are introduced to our children at primary school level.

To win the war on illiteracy and search for a common language, we and our people's government are to respect our school teachers and make their working environment conducive. We are to make them love and enjoy their profession so that they stick to their career and work hard. That way our education sector will play its very important role in the development of our nation. And like any other aspect of our national development, addressing these two critical national issues should be informed by our national principles of justice for all, liberty for all, prosperity for all, equality for all, fear and love of God as well as our love for one another.

Summary

The national wealth ahead of us is more vast than what we have encountered so far since 2005. It is waiting beneath and above our motherland to enrich all of us. But if we focus on quarrelling and fighting among ourselves because of the compatatively less wealth that is believed to have been squandered selfishly by some of us, we will forfeit both the current and future riches of our nation. As a result, others will benefit from it and encourage us to keep fighting and killing ourselves while they go on looting our resources and tearing down our nation. Now, the choice is ours, we the South Sudanese people, to forgive our brothers and sisters who might have taken some of our common wealth and directed it to their private use or hound them to a deadly end. Can't we learn from our past so as to know what to do to be able to benefit from the present and be guided in seeking a brighter future? To me, for the sake of our dear nation as well as our current and future generation and our unity, we ought to forgive and ask them to return the funds while exploring ways of avoiding dangerous pitfalls in future. Meanwhile, we must direct our time, energy and material resources to good use so as to establish good control systems immediately to safeguard our present and future. Forgiveness is biblical and the best solution to any interpersonal problems under the sun.

For the sake of our national cohesion, and in order to help our citizens to exploit their potential, learn their rights and how to protect them as they participate in national building, our government should urgently address illiteracy and language problem in South Sudan. We should have a national, unified language of communication. We must fight illiteracy by availing to all our people basic education. If the high level of illiteracy and lack of common language among our people persists, even good government programmes will not take off, and the nation will remain bogged down by tribalism, poverty, civil strife, disease, suspicion, misinformation, etc. Let us be experts in identifying and fighting our common enemies!

Chapter Four

THE SEARCH FOR NATIONAL UNITY

Introduction

A decentralized system of government can be good, but only if it comes after people have been under a centralized system long enough to have become unified. That time devolution is justified, since it is necessitated by the need to give better services, and it will not divide citizens. But if it comes before people attain a high level of cohesion and patriotism, it may divide them along tribal lines and by the areas they come from. Today, the main issue facing our young nation of South Sudan is not the need to decentralize and polarize our already divided people; rather, it is how to unite them.

Any created thing, be it living or inanimate, has its own attraction or repulsive features. It may be beautiful or ugly, strong or weak, big or small, toxic or non-poisonous, sweet or bitter, friendly or unfriendly, kind or unkind, long-lasting or short-lived, rich or poor, hot or cold—the list is very long. It may have some features that make it seem good or fairly appealing.

It is universally accepted that people prefer certain moral features and dislike others. The positive moral features that most people appreciate include goodness, beauty, strength, honesty, love, kindness, creativity, richness, generousity, reliability, wisdom, understanding, forgiveness and peace, just to name a few. But some people who are given to moral deviance tend to admire some negative moral features such as dishonesty, hatred, unkindness, laziness, meanness, unfriendliness, being unsocial and selfishness, among others. Some people like to give to and receive from others, but others love only to receive from others but give to none.

Culture is a philosophy of life and a choice through which a person or a group of people acquire, adopt and develop certain behavioural characteristics which, with the passage of time, govern their conduct in life. Sometimes people may be subjected to such behaviour by external forces in their context. As a result, they are left without an option but to adopt, develop and own those unique characteristics to define their culture. If such behaviour enables them to attain their personal or collective goals, they will cherish and encourage others to live by it, irrespective of whether outsiders like or dislike it. That explains why wife inheritance, male circumcision and sharing of one wife by biological brothers, among others traditions, have survived the passage of time in certain parts of the world.

There are no people with a superior culture that other human beings can copy and own or take as a yardstick for evaluating other cultures. This is because the best in one culture may be the worst in another, and vice versa. But Christians are guided by a culture that transcends human cultures, God's culture that is defined in the Bible.

There are two things worth mentioning here. First, human culture is dynamic, as it is continuously influenced by social changes, economic changes, political changes, and religious and environmental changes. As part and parcel of human life, culture changes to adapt to other changes for life to continue under the sun. Second, the best human civilization is basically a culture that has been modified to adapt to changes in its environment. In such a case, you retain your culture, discard bad aspects of your own culture but selectively adopt admirable aspects of other cultures.

For instance, the Dinka people have now realized that the traditional facial scars and removal of lower teeth do not serve a useful purpose in this age; hence, most of their young people are managing well without having to go through such painful experiences. The Dinkas have been forced to modify or improve on the forms of cultural initiation without necessarily discarding the rite of passage altogether. But there are aspects of modern culture to avoid. Unfortunately, there are people who do away completely with their own culture and adopt everything of another culture. People should know that all human cultures are relative; there is no single human culture under the sun that is absolute.

Every nation has the culture that defines it. Some cultures produce peaceful, loving, tolerant, kind, understanding, and wise people, just to name a few. Others, on the other hand, produce aggressive, uncaring, violent, mean, unfriendly and selfish people. Yet these are extremes; the cultures of most nations lie between these two extremes. The behaviour of people adjusts itself to meet changing conditions.

National culture is nothing more than the culture of most

people in that nation. After all it is people who make up the nation. So if the culture of the people is morally good and humane, then their national culture will be the same.

Before the advent of today's global community of nations, people in different countries were content with their unique cultures. This is because, first, interaction between communities was minimal as a result of which every one considered their culture best, for there was no benchmarking. Second, as international laws were not yet in place to prevent human rights violation, people used their own cultural laws to protect themselves and their possessions and sometimes to forcefully acquire resources and oppress others. As long as a people's culture was able to make them realise their personal and collective aspirations, be it at the expense of others, the owners of the culture were happy with it.

But with the advent of globalization and the crafting of international policies and laws that protect human rights, regressive cultures are now forced to change so as to be in line with the demands of today. Archaic cultures that condone oppression have no place in the world of today. Those who cling to such old-fashioned cultures risk being shunned or isolated by the modernists.

The modernisation of human cultures has seen the abolition of slavery, formulation and implementation of international laws that led to the creation of the International Criminal Court to check excesses in governance by dealing with people accused of committing war crimes and crimes against humanity. These days, people do not just do bad things, even locally, and imagine they will get away with it. The conception of democratic and socialist principles of governance is also a part of these cultural developments.

In the case of the newly established Republic of South

Sudan, national culture consists of a unique blend of 64 cultural aspects. These aspects can be grouped into five dimensions of a personality, namely openness, extraversion, neuroticism, conscientious and agreeableness. Or, to use other terms concerning personality, they can be categorized into sanguine, phlegmatic, choleric or melancholic. But if I were to go further and categorize our national culture into two major divisions, it turns out that it is made up of extraverted and introverted patterns.

These cultural categorizations are good if they are used flexibly to complement and enhance each other. But if they are rigidly allowed to compete with each other within the same culture, these components will tear their own culture apart, and there will be a kind of personality clash within the national culture.

The purpose of this chapter is to make our people see the need to halt the call for decentralization and instead look for ways of becoming more cohesive under the existing system of government. The purpose of this chapter is also to find out how to harmonize our 64 ethnic cultures for synergy as we seek to come up with one great national culture. This culture will bring unity among our people since it will emphasize fear and love of God and love of each other, thus enabling us realize justice for all, liberty for all, prosperity for all and equality for all. Early decentralization of our people may benefit in a few ways, but not in national unity.

How to Unite the South Sudanese

The people of South Sudan, comprising 64 ethnic groups, have been living as separate communities with no way of uniting them from time immemorial. This state of affairs was reinforced by the fact that communication was minimal. Even as recently as the late nineteenth century, it was very rare for one to move from Bor to Mangalla, a distance of about 100 miles. Actually, if one did travel that far and returned home safely, this merited the performance of rituals and sacrifices. I am told that Anyieth Jangdit, the father of the retired Bishop Nathaniel Garang, went to Yirol area from Bor one day in search of something. Upon his arrival there, people asked him whether the earth ends in Bor, and they were surprised to hear that it extends beyond there. This shows that even different clans within the same tribe had least contact with each other.

Even during the time of colonialism, little effort was made to unite the Southerners. What forced them for the first time to pursue a common goal and hence, interacted with each other more in the process was their first civil war, the Anyanya Movement. Even then, most soldiers fought from their specific geographical locations. As such, there was no noticeable unity among our different communities.

After the end of the Anyanya War and the establishment of the Juba Government in 1972, the Southerners started to live and work together in the public or private sectors, especially in urban areas. Schools came to represent the face of South Sudan in that they had children from different ethnic backgrounds. I, for example, got my early education in St. Joseph Primary and Buluk Intermediate School in Juba and Rumbek Secondary in Rumbek where I studied with children from other different communities. Government officials were assigned, depending on their competence and other considerations, to serve the public in different parts of South Sudan. For instance, the first Commissioner of Jonglei Province was Banensio Loro from Bari Community near Juba. The late Ajith Awuol from Bor one time served as Commissioner of Lakes Province.

Over time, common members of different communities also started to move and interact freely. Henceforth, it became a common feature to see the Murles with their animals in Bor during the dry season, searching for water and pastures along the Nile. Bor, the capital of Jonglei Province, became a melting pot, with all the different tribes from Jonglei who came there for training and to look for job opportunities relating to their different areas of specialization.

Because of unrestricted movement of the Southerners, some people from Bor ventured beyond to other regions such as Mangalla and Juba. Some of them kept animals and others started small businesses or did menial jobs. As their income dictated, most of those people ended up living in slums in and around Juba. One such place is known as Thongpiny. 'Thongpiny' is a combination of two words in Dinka, 'thoŋ' and 'piny'. 'Thoŋ' means alike and 'piny' means place or earth. Hence, Thongpiny means the place is alike, suggesting that people from different communities lived together here in unity. Yes, as the name suggests, people from different tribes started to live in Juba, engaging in all manner of work and businesses.

At this time, the Southerners were unconsciously building their common identity that transcended their ethnic differences and people's station in life. It was this unity that started early among the Southerners that led the students and people of other walks of life to demonstrate against government plans and policies in connection with the Jonglei Canal and border revision by Khartoum Government in an effort to annex sections of South Sudan that were endowed with natural resources and make them part of North Sudan.

Seeing this growing unity among the Southerners as a potential threat to their long-range plans to gain complete control of South Sudan and plunder it, the Khartoum

Government divided the united Southern Regional Autonomy into three regions, namely: Equatoria, Upper Nile and Bhar el Ghazal. Although some of our gullible people thought this division was meant to improve governance and the giving of services, it was actually a way of forestalling the growing and healthy unity among Southerners; its hidden objective was to turn brethren against each other. That is how the same people came to view themselves as being from "Great Upper Nile", "Great Bhar el Ghazal", or "Great Equatoria". But what is great about these flattering names? Hasn't this division been an intelligent way of causing disunity among the sons and daughters of the same mother and setting the stage for a senseless war? What pride can be derived from this division when it has caused our motherland to overflow with the blood of her sons and daughters as they kill each other in a war caused by disunity?

Divisive Khartoum policies led to the second more bloody and protracted civil war in Sudan that began in 1983 and ended in 2005. Faced with a common enemy, the Southerners once again embraced unity to fight the war of liberation, though the unhealthy spirit of division followed some, making them leave the common enemy and turn their weapons against their own people. Unlike the time of Anyanya One, the long period of SPLA/M struggle made the Southerners gain more understanding of themselves, becoming a more cohesive group. This is because people fought and died anywhere, not just on their own soil but sometimes in other marginalized areas in North Sudan. Henceforth, they began to view themselves as Southerners, fighting and dying anywhere and for a common cause. The war brought the people together.

But after they won the war and got their dear independence, our people, unfortunately, recoiled into their ethnic and regional cocoons. The division among the sons and daughters of the same land became even deeper and more acrimonious than at the time of Kokoro (Division) in 1983. This time the disunity found expression in "The Decentralization System of Government." So far, the former three regions have given birth to ten states. Now as I write, there are some people in these states who are pushing for further division of the nation to have 21 or more states. As if that is not enough trouble, still others are calling for a federal government in South Sudan. If the latter is accepted, God knows what these people will demand for next!

There is nothing bad about a decentralized system of governance if it results in a more equitable sharing of the nation's resources and makes marginalized sections of the nation experience development also. But a decentralized system of government has another side to it: it does not enhance unity among people if such people had not experienced strong cohesion as a nation before, something people of our new nation of South Sudan are yet to experience. Instead of bringing people together, decentralization often brings about rifts, as people's loyalty is shifted to the new divisions they begin to identify with. Its results are even worse if it is adopted and implemented by selfish people whose intention is to reject others and live in isolation.

Today in South Sudan, apart from maybe the armed forces and the people working for national government, people are divided by bumas, payams, counties and states. Besides being divided along tribal line, our people are even divided by clans within the same tribe sometimes. In the case of Greater Bor, for instance, the Commissioner of Bor County is and must be from Bor; the Commissioner of Twic East County is and must be from Twic, and the Commissioner of Duk is and must always be from there.

The idea of a decentralized system of government has surprisingly won the hearts of many, even in the church in South Sudan, for most of them operate in places of their origin. Yet this is a critical period in the history of our young nation, which calls for church leaders to act as the salt and the light among our people, as required of them by the Lord Jesus Christ. So far, people have been identifying their spiritual leaders by their tribes and the areas they come from.

Except tertiary colleges and universities, children in lower classes attend school where parents live and work. This is another negative sign of decentralization, creating division among the people right from their childhood. Let me now leave the advantages of a decentralized system of government to highlight some of the well-known disadvantages here below.

First, unity will give way to disunity. The little unity that our people have managed to forge in the past will automatically and systematically go, since there will be nothing to bring people together. And as usual, a divided people are a weak people.

Second, the spirit of nationalism will give way to the spirit of tribalism and regionalism. When people work and live together, they value and depend on one another, despite their differences. As they live, work and move together, they cease to see themselves as individuals with loyalty to their ethnic groups and regions and begin to view themselves as belonging to a bigger and more important entity, their nation. This is the beginning of true nationalism. Before we get to this point, we will remain in the realm of fear, selfishness, hatred and jealousy that characterize those who identify with tribe rather than with our great nation of South Sudan.

Third, we will continue to view each other suspiciously as if we are enemies, despite living within the four corners of our nation where we are protected by our armed forces. A nation whose people are suspicious of each other and wrongly view each other as enemies is an uncomfortable country to live and work in because such people are like atomic bomb, ready to explode at the least provocation. Love, freedom and joy do not inhabit such tense environments. Citizens of the same motherland should live and work together as brothers and sisters and learn to resolve any differences with love. It is only when people live, work and share their joy and sorrow together that they allay their fears and view each other as true friends. Unity never exists in an environment of suspicion and animosity.

Forth, people will keep dividing themselves endlessly until they reach a level of indivisibility in their specific tribes and localities. And every sub-division is an additional nail to the coffin of national cohesion.

Fifth, decentralization will require that people be employed by their local governments. This will hamper the giving of services by civil servants because it is not always possible to serve your own people without being accused of favoritism. People who know you are difficult to work with, and you rarely rise to your potential when you work near home. Indeed, Jesus Christ warned: 'I tell you the truth…no prophet is accepted in his own town" (Lk.4:24). People of his town of Nazareth failed to benefit from his miracles like people of other regions because of familiarity and criticism of him. Similarly, civil servants tend to be ignored when they work among their own people and therefore, become demoralized. In the long run, they are accused of failing in their work by the same people who contributed to their failure.

Sixth, national leaders will be biased as they allocate resources, for they will direct more resources to the places where they have vested interests. This will result in unfair distribution of national services. The result will be happy and unhappy people within the same nation.

Seventh, people of different areas will envy and hate one another. This is so because when resources in some areas are explored and extracted and others left unexploited or they have nothing to exploit, some regions will be wealthy and others will lag behind. Then there will be no ways of helping people from poor regions. This will be another blow to national unity.

Eighth, as some people live in affluence and others in poverty, the resulting animosity will prevent them from standing together in defence of their nation in the event of aggression. Moreover, the nation will internally be riddled with civil strife.

Ninth, the children of the rich and the children of the poor will not integrate well when they go for higher education, since they will attend different schools for their early education. This problem will be compounded by the fact that most children drop from school before getting to university. Thus, unity among our children will be dealt a blow.

Tenth, God will not be happy if his church conforms to the world rather than changing it. He will be even more displeased if the church happens to contribute to polarization rather than being a solution to the problems facing our people.

Eleventh, but those are not the only challenges of decentralization. A decentralized system of government calls for more personnel to implement and manage it than a centralized one. As a result, the government wage bill normally becomes bloated, leaving little or no funds for services and development.

But what can we do as the people of South Sudan to stem

the current tide? To me, we are faced with a grave national issue that requires our collective thinking and measures to address it. But allow me to express my thoughts so far as the issue is concerned.

First, there are many who value this current system of government and can attest to its benefits. That is one reason to let it continue as for now.

Second, decentralization will call for further decentralization, resulting in the undesirable consequences of a young nation like ours having to fund a big government. So we should rethink what we are calling for to avoid being a fragmented people and pauperizing our nation to pay a huge wage bill as we sacrifice development.

Third, if decentralization and further decentralization is necessitated by unfair distribution of national cake, then let all of us appreciate and use our core principles of justice for all, liberty for all, prosperity for all, equality for all, fear and love of God as well as love for one another when it comes to sharing resources. That way, we will live in unity. Let us pursue what unites us and shun what divides us.

Fourth, let our church and other religious groups take a completely neutral position and act as the salt and the light of the young nation of South Sudan so as to keep our people united. A time has come for the spiritual leaders to prove that they are nationalists by calling upon their flocks to rise above narrow ethnic and regional interests and bring national interests to the fore.

Fifth, state governors, county commissioners, high school principals and other senior government officials should be deployed to states and counties outside where they are born so that they can be more effective in their work. There should also be rotation. For instance, one could work in one state or county for two years or so and then shift to another place before the next general elections take place. The people's leader will shoulder this noble task with the help of his policymakers. This will enable such people to exploit their potential fully and benefit all parts of the nation. At the same time, doing this will bring unity among the people.

Sixth, if staff of our law-enforcing agencies comprise our sons and daughters drawn from different parts of our nation and are deployed in different parts of the nation and rotated on a regular basis, their loyalty will ultimately shift from their ethnic groups and regions to the nation. For example, supposing a policeman who happens to be a Dinka from and working in Yirol is taken and assigned to work in Kapoeta, will he have any role to play in local politics? No. Hence, he will not be biased in discharging his national duty. But if he remains in Yirol, it will be hard avoiding to be dragged into local politics. And he will do this at the expense of national duty. Stationing a man or woman of gun in one place for long can also create unnecessary problems, especially during this time of national building.

Seventh, our government should come up with national schools to be founded in every state, including the national capital, whose curriculum is aimed at inculcating patriotism and unity in the minds of our young people. Investing in these well-trained future leaders will be a way of ensuring that there will always be people who are pushing for togetherness in our nation.

Eighth, church leaders too should be rotated. They should not be confined to shepherding people in their places of birth or among people who speak their vernacular. This is because even if they don't have a divisive spirit and tend to love their flocks as themselves, what befell Jesus Christ may happen to them, too. And when there is a local problem, others will find it hard to distinguish their thoughts and actions from those of their kinsmen. If they are transferred and made to work anywhere in South Sudan, they will help unite our people.

Ninth, the call for unity among our people should be constantly broadcast in the media and other channels of communication. This call should be mainstreamed in the education system and conveyed through any other means.

Tenth, we should honour and love one another, the weak and the strong, the young and the old, the rich and the poor, male and female, for God knows why he brought us together as one nation.

Eleventh, we should shun those who divide us and support those who unite us.

Let's begin with the importance of unity in diversity.

The Importance of Unity in Diversity

Rainbow becomes what it is because of its beautiful colours. Birds and animals, fish and other creatures, big or small, weak or strong, grace our landscape, attracting tourists and hence, foreign currency. The mountainous countryside with its uneven hills is a very attractive sight. Different colours and sizes of clouds make the sky amazing to look at during the day, while various heavenly bodies declare the glory of the Creator throughout the night. Consequently, no one can resist looking up to see them. The Creator of the universe had every reason to make His creatures the way it pleased him, and he expects them to appreciate, love, enjoy and complement their unique, diverse characteristics.

This is not always the case with human beings, the ones created in the Creator's own image and likeness. Beginning right from the untimely death of Abel in the hands of his own unkind brother Cain, man has been expressing hatred, causing divisions and destroying fellow human beings mercilessly. Sometimes, the mere difference in the colour of one's skin has been used to justify racialism between the sons and daughters of the same father and mother, Adam and Eve. What man fails to appreciate is the fact that different skin colours are meant to enrich the beauty of creation. Even the soil has different colours.

Birds of the air love and appreciate their different colours. Land animals and fish love and appreciate their unique colours. Trees and other plants appreciate their different colours. Roses have different colours and even thorns.

Disliking himself has been the main cause of man's own destruction and the widespread destruction of other creatures upon the earth. For example, he has been waging ruthless wars against himself from time immemorial. The results of such wars are numerous. These include enslavement and oppression of man by man. Since ancient times, man has been building civilizations after civilizations but later destroying them. Even today it has taken caring world leaders to protect the current civilization from destruction by man himself. Man is his own worst enemy; he is the one who has made the world to be an unfavourable place to live in.

Now the question to ask ourselves is: why does man hate and destroy himself and the other creatures under the sun? I cannot provide a satisfactory answer to this age-old question. But allow me to attempt an answer, assisted by my imagination. First, the problem that originally led man to leave his first habitation, the Garden of Eden, is the same one that led to the shedding of Abel's blood by his evil brother Cain. This problem gave birth to man's moral degradation that is characterised by greed, hatred, jealousy, envy, unfaithfulness, dishonesty, unkindness, selfishness, self-destruction, dissension and factions, just to name a few. Biblically, these and many other examples of moral depravity are called the acts of the flesh or sinful nature. They have been enslaving and destroying man and other creatures since the time he left the Garden of Eden.

As Christians teach, for man to achieve a complete moral paradigm shift, he has to return to his Creator through the only door that has been sacrificially opened by Jesus Christ. This is by accepting him as their Lord and Saviour. I say 'the only door' because Jesus Himself in the Word of God says, 'I am the way and the truth and the life. No one comes to the Father except through me' (Jn.14:6).

With this new belief comes the indwelling of man by his Creator. This union restores man's lost morality so that he ceases to be enslaved by his crooked nature. For Paul says: "… If anyone is in Christ, he is a new creation; the old has gone, the new has come!" (2Cor.5:19). A person who is in Christ is not reformed, rehabilitated or re-educated; he is recreated and indwelt by Christ through the power of the Holy Spirit. Henceforth, his carnal behaviour gives way to the fruit of the Spirit, which is love, joy, peace, patience, kindness, goodness, faithfulness, gentleness and self-control (Gal.5:22-23). Such a person is said to have crucified the sinful nature with its passions and desires.

Whether we are Christians, Muslims, animists, communists, secularists, humanists, I strongly believe no person in his right mind fault seeking to be guided by the nine ingredients of the fruit of the Spirit. Since these spiritual attributes—joy, peace, patience, kindness, goodness, faithfulness, gentleness and self-control—are what make life good and worth living, they make people live and work together as brothers and sisters.

It is the moral duty of our people in South Sudan to shun what divides, dehumanises and destroys them and disgraces God. Instead, they are to cherish, uphold and safeguard what dignifies them, what is humane and glorifies their God.

Summary

There are successful nations with decentralized forms of government like the US and West Germany, but they decentralized many years after becoming a united people through a centralized system of government. Genuine decentralization is provoked by growth of the economy and the attendant desire to improve services through devolution. Decentralizing shortly after independence is therefore, unjustified and could dash the dream of ever becoming a united nation. A nation is rather like a family in many ways, and one must live together with his children in the same house for many years as they are nurtured before they go separate ways to form their own families. History has shown that any nation must first unite her citizens and decentralize later, if need be. If people opt for division before they have experienced unity, then it is clear they will not be doing so for the sake of improving services to the people but because they reject and hate each other.

The Lord has blessed South Sudan with a host of ethnic groups. They have rich cultures; they are powerful warriors; they have men and women with the gift of the garb; some of their people are wise; they have godly and humane men and women; they have peace lovers; they have hardworking people; they are jealous of their motherland. The list of moral attributes of our people is very long. But as human beings, they have their own weaknesses as well.

No one culture will make South Sudan good. Every culture ought to contribute what is good about it and it be used to make our nation strong and attractive to outsiders. I have my weak and strong points and you have your weak and strong points, so we need each other to survive. We should appreciate our similarities and differences, for they complement each other. Let us appreciate each other's strengths and weaknesses. We should oppose what divides us and appreciate what unites us. Unity in diversity should be the cornerstone of the nation of South Sudan. Unity in diversity shold be one of the roots of our esteemed nation. Collectively, minus our undesirable cultural aspects, all South Sudanese cultures can make one admirable national culture.

In order for us to promote unity among our people within the current system of government, our government should come up with some acceptable plans and policies and implement them intentionally and systematically. Such policies should meet individual and collective aspirations of all Southerners. In promoting national unity, the involvement of senior government officials, church and other religious leaders and all members of the armed forces should be sought. If we mean what we say and say what we mean and do what we mean and say, the young nation of South Sudan will emerge as a united country where people live and work in harmony.

Chapter Five

THE ROOTS OF
NATIONAL
SELF-ESTEEM

Introduction

For us and our nation to experience valuable self-esteem, we are to respect human life, senior citizens, the disadvantaged citizens, national leaders, women and youth and members of the armed forces. We must also respect our widows and widowers, orphans and single ladies and our public wealth. Our self-respect must be a vital root of our national pride. We are to respect aliens, our national law, government and politics. Also for us to boost our national image, we must share our national cake equitably and promote religious tolerance, forgiveness and good neighbourliness. That way we will maximise our friends and minimise our enemies. Discussed here also is the importance of the protection of national environment.

Respect for Citizens, Aliens and Others

Respect is not to be demanded. If you demand it from people, they will give it to you out of fear. But that respect is short-lived. True respect is earned by the person himself through his good deeds, words and noble thoughts.

Then other people will value and bestow respect upon him. If he defaults on it, people will immediately withdraw it from him. Then it will be very hard for him to acquire it once more, for people will be very cautious to hurry in, placing their respect on him for the second time. In other words, respect is very expensive yet difficult to earn and retain for longer period of time, and when it is lost, it is very, very hard to regain.

People who have no respect for one another do not enjoy living, eating and working together. They don't love each other; they hate and fight each other. Respect for all our national citizens should be one of the primary objectives in South Sudan. Our respect for one another is very important. We should respect one other despite our difference in age, gender, socio-economic status, political affiliation, or religious, geographic and ethnic backgrounds. Respect can be counted on as a reliable factor in the building of our national foundation.

In this section of the book, we will explore the importance of respect for human life, whether the life of the senior and disadvantaged citizens, national leaders, women, youths or armed forces. For the love of God and other people, we will also look into the importance of respecting aliens.

Respect for Human Life

Human life is sacred. Our Creator made man—male and female—in his own image and likeness and breathed his life into him. This is what sets human beings apart from other creatures. Man's life is more important in God's eyes than the life of any animal, whether bird, fish or any other living creature that moves on the ground. That is why Abel's blood cried to God from the ground after his death in the hands of his unkind brother Cain (Gen.4:4b), as a result of which God punished Cain for murdering his brother by cursing the ground and making him a wanderer. Every other person is important, and that is why God commands man not to kill.

Human life is more important than any amount of money or herds of cattle. Even when people pay for or accept some cattle or money as compensation for people who have been killed (a common practice in certain cultures), this is just an expression of sorrowing with those who have lost their loved ones, for human life is too valuable to attach monetary value to it. And it doesn't matter whether it is the life of a male or female, old or young, poor or rich, educated or uneducated, a wise person or a fool, wholesome or disabled. Life is life in the eyes of God.

In most of the South Sudanese communities, human life was and is still considered highly valuable; it is actually regarded as sacred. Here if a person kills anyone intentionally or unintentionally, he is made to face full force of the law. Even if the culprit is not himself killed, he has to undergo some cleansing rites to appease God so that he does not avenge the shed blood, making the community suffer. Unfortunately, lack of respect for human life, characterized by the deliberate killing of human beings, has become common in many parts of our nation.

South Sudan is regarded as a religious country since almost all her citizens consist of Christians, Muslims and followers of traditional deities. But I wonder whether there is any one of those faiths whose teaching supports disrespect for human life or the deliberate shedding of human blood. If that were so with any faith, then it is the high time its teachings were revised so that adherents start to embrace respect for human life for the sake of our national cohesion, brotherly love and fear of God.

If you value and respect your life as a human being, why don't you value and respect someone else's life? Human life is too dear to waste, for there is always a divine purpose for such a life being on earth.

For God to bless our new nation and for people of other nations to respect us, respect for human life should first be made one of the principles upon which to build our nation. Even when we are boiling with anger and tempted to seek revenge, we could become mollified by choosing to see human life through God's eyes. Our nation should be known for genuine respect for human life, whether it is the life of a citizen of South Sudan or of an alien.

Respect for Senior Citizens

Grey hair is as precious as gold and as elusive as holding air in your hand. It is not obtained by human effort but bestowed by the Giver of life. Any community or nation that has senior citizens is highly blessed by God, for they are the receptacles of their traditional lore to be handed down to their children for onward transmission to their children's children. Old people have seen all of life; so they have what it takes to guard the innocent.

For the purpose of this book, let me refer to our parents as senior citizens, for there is no the former in the absence of the latter – parents and senior citizens mean the same thing. And as we pay due respect to our own biological parents, we should do the same to all our senior citizens. Indeed, if you have not been honouring them, start doing that right now!

I know some people don't respect their own parents, sometimes even wishing them quick departure from this world. But what they fail to appreciate is that the path of old age is a universal one for all living creatures. So if you don't respect but instead wish others to hurry along and leave the scene, others will also compel you to do the same when you grow old.

The current disrespect and fear of old age has made some people to continue behaving young, even dyeing their heads to camouflage greying hair. Others are closely shaven to hide receding hairline and grey hair. Yet this will not completely remove their age-related physical changes like the creasing of the skin. So let us accept and enjoy our old age, for this is an unavoidable stage of life for all of us except those who die young.

Apostle Paul has a word of wisdom for us in this connection: "Children, obey your parents in the Lord, for this is right. 'Honour your father and mother'—which is the first commandment with a promise—'that it will go well with you and that you may enjoy long life on the earth' (Eph.6:1-3). As we see in this quotation, respect for senior citizens brings God's blessings upon individuals and the whole nation in general. When they are disrespected and mishandled, they leave the world saddened and thus, curse instead of blessing us.

Therefore, as a people we should seek to give the due, and sometimes undeserved respect, to all our senior citizens, both the ones we are related to and others. We should not shun but respect and care for them as they journey through life to the world of no return. Moreover, so long as they are still capable physically and mentally, senior citizens should be engaged both at local and national levels, unless they themselves expressly say that they are not ready to work. Respect for our senior citizens should be one of the moral obligations in our nation.

Respect for Disadvantaged Citizens

There is no single community or nation under the sun that has no disabled people, since physical or mental disability is a part of life. Some people are born with disabilities, but others acquire disability along the rough path of life. Some disabilities are somewhat mild, but others are very serious and life threatening.

Our young nation of South Sudan has a huge number of war victims and therefore, many crippled, blind and deaf people. But there are still people with other forms of disabilities. Most of these now disadvantaged citizens got their physical and mental defects in the course of our fight for independence, and we cannot afford to ignore them, considering the sacrifice they paid to deliver to this generation an independent country.

There are two primary things that we must appreciate about our esteemed but disadvantaged citizens:

First, it is common knowledge that disability is not inability. Let me give an amazing illustration to support this truth. In Nairobi in May 2014, I watched a live programme on TV, featuring a Kenyan young lady who was born with no arms. But in the course of time, after refusing to accept this natural challenge, she made her legs start to serve her in more ways than just walking. These other ways included writing, washing, cooking, cleaning, bathing, holding things and greeting people. She even got herself a good education, married a young man, and they have a handsome baby boy. Is that not a great achievement, considering the many odds against her? In some cultures, that beautiful, happy child of God would have been dumped and abandoned before seeing her second day after birth.

There are schools for the blind, and some of the blind people are far more endowed than those who see with their two eyes. I have a good friend of mine by the name John Kuol from ECS Diocese of Bor. He is blind but educated and also acquired carpentry skills in Kenya in the 1990s. He has even trained himself to walk without a guide, cultivates land and does many other things by himself. He is capable of identifying every one of his close relatives and acquaintances by voice and touch of hand. He is married and has a good family. These are indication of the fact that disability is not inability.

Second, to be disabled physically or mentally does not necessarily mean that such a person's life is not useful. The life of a disabled person is the same as the life of the person who is whole. In God's eyes, his life is as precious as any other person's life. Both the disabled and people who are without disabilities all belong to God. At death, our graves will look the same. Life is life, and at death, grave is grave. Even the life of a person who is both mute and deaf is still very precious in God's sight.

In March 2014, I travelled to Juba from Nairobi, Kenya, on my way to Bor. Some friends picked me at the airport and took me to a place in town to spend the night. At some point the driver took a turn and joined a rough lane to avoid the roundabout at Juba University. After asking my friends the reason for doing this, they told me the road was blocked by some demonstrating disabled soldiers. When I asked why the soldiers were demonstrating, one of my friends said, "These disabled soldiers are disturbing people". He went on to explain that they had gone for three months without their monthly allowances and that this is what they were pressing for from the government.

Disagreeing with his view that these soldiers were disturbing the public, I told my friend that as any other citizen, the soldiers had a right to show their dissatisfaction with the way their government was doing things, as long as their demonstration was peaceful. "We would do the same or even worse had we been in their position," I added.

For a national cause, some people risk to be killed, crippled, blinded, or detained so that their fellow countrymen live healthy lives, work and enjoy with their families. Don't you think that such people deserve our respect and love, even if mental torture at the battlefront has affected some mentally, making them at times uncontrollable?

For the sake of our national pride and for the sake of humanity and fear of God, our disabled citizens should be respected and their interests upheld and protected by all the South Sudanese people. Let this be one of the moral values that our young nation will be known for. And for this, rest assured that the loving and merciful God will bless our land abundantly.

Respect for National Leaders

Who should lead, and who should follow? Any human being is capable of leading as well as following. There is no one who has never been a leader or a follower in his life. All of us are born to lead and follow others at one time or other. Moreover, we should appreciate the fact that at some point, some people develop certain weaknesses in leading or following others. But generally, no one has ever led people under the sun without making any mistake.

Leadership, even at the family level, is not a simple job, since dealing with people is not as easy as dealing with dumb creatures. I say this for a couple of reasons. First, human beings, low or high, think. They are also critical and are jealous and rebellious because of the inherent Adamic nature. Their first parents rebelled, and they too are still rebelling against God and those he has put in leadership. Of course, human leadership could be flawed, making those who are being led to be justified in disobeying and rebelling against the leader for not discharging his mandate satisfactorily. But even when people are being led well, some may still oppose the leader because of their own ulterior motives.

Second, those outside the "Situation Room" sometimes use their subjective evaluations to rate the leader and reach biased conclusions about him and his rule. They imagine themselves better replacements of their ruler. But even if some of them may be better leaders than the current ruler, subjecting themselves to someone else's leadership is in keeping with the fact that leaders always lead other leaders. Moreover, it is common knowledge that the harshest critics in a dance are often the poorest dancers.

Third, a leader is just like any other human being: as a person, he has strengths and weaknesses. A leader could perform well or mess up; he is susceptible to sinful temptations and yielding to human pressure. A leader could be vengeful as he deals with his subjects. He has his own family and other things to attend to...the list of the things that could negatively influence one's leadership can be quite long.

Very often, people pay close attention to the weaknesses of their leader more than his strengths. Actually, if we were to use an objective behavioural scale to evaluate the deeds, words and thoughts of a normal person, we will be surprised to discover that such a person's goodness outweighs his badness. All people do more good things than bad things in life. So if a person is too bad to do good, then he is too bad to live in this world. Yet such a person would not to blame entirely because he shares the same nature with us, the depraved nature inherited from Adam. What is to blame is that bad spirit in him that makes him too morally bad.

Having established that a normal person does more good things than bad things in life, what do you think about any leader in this world? I believe if we gave him a fair rating, his moral excellence would be above his moral failings. There is no way in which those who are morally good will choose one of theirs who happens to be, in their evaluation, morally imbalanced or too bad to lead them. Under normal circumstances, any leader of the people is placed in power by his people after being perceived to have some admirable, undeniable leadership qualities that make him stand taller than others among his people. If the leader is morally too bad to lead, then the simple, logical conclusion is that his followers are morally worse.

There are many reasons why people should love and respect their leader. First, any leader, be it a class monitor, a school headmaster, a chairperson of a committee, a church leader, a trade union leader, the leader of a military junta, an army commander, the leader of a theocracy, or even a democratically elected leader is, in the first place, given the leadership authority by his own people. And they do this with great rejoicing. Besides, by accepting to lead them, he actually puts his own life on the line, sacrifices time with his own family and his private aspirations to serve his people. Sometimes he may die in the course of serving his followers.

So if he makes some mistakes, whether big or small, while leading his people, they should not be blamed entirely on him. His followers are also to blame because they are the ones who enthroned him in the first place. Yet it is common knowledge that people enjoy benefits accruing from their leader's good decisions but will not bear with his failures. If we really love and appreciate a leader's services, we are duty bound to respect him and overlook his mistakes, knowing that we are the ones who allowed him to have rule over us in the first place.

Second, it is biblical to forgive one another, including our worst enemies. Jesus Christ admonishes us to love our enemies and pray for those who persecute us (Matt.5:44). If we forgive and respect our leader, he will love and respect us in return, and the kindness shown to him may bring about the desired change in his character. Then the Lord will bless all of us.

Third, if we respect and forgive our leader of any sorts of moral shortcomings, he is sure to do the same to us his followers whenever we err. If you respect and forgive the leader today, he will do the same to you tomorrow.

Fourth, if we respect our leader, we and our nation will reap abundant blessings from God. This is because there will be harmony existing between us and our leader, which will lead to a peaceful atmosphere within our nation and attract God's blessings. God loves to dwell where there is peace.

Fifth, it is an abomination that could lead to the nation being cursed for a leader to die and be buried outside his homeland. It is equally bad for people to kill their own leader, despite the adverse effects of the mistakes made during his rule. This is because he will have made those mistakes inadvertently in the course of leading his own people.

It is my personal wish that all our leaders in South Sudan should lead, live, die and be buried with full respect at home, irrespective of their poor or good judgments during their leadership. It is better to shame one of your own, especially a leader, at home than to disgrace him in the eyes of outsiders who will in turn scornfully laugh at you.

If we respect our leaders, this will be an indication that we love one another and love God. It also expresses our maturity as a people. If we exhibit humane, respectful attitude towards our leaders, other nations will respect and love our leaders, our nation and us. Respect for leaders is one of the highest indicators of a self-respecting nation.

Respect for Women

First of all, men and women are equal in the eyes of God, both having been created in His own image and likeness. The Lord made them to complement each other and procreate until they fill the world and dominate all other creatures on earth. In the Bible, the term "man" is generic, being used to refer to both male and female. And that is how I apply the term in my writings. Indeed, the Bible says, "When God created man, he made him in the likeness of God. He created them male and female and blessed them. And when they were created, he called them 'man' (Gen.5:1-2). God expects them to love and respect one another.

When it comes to procreation, the woman carries a heavier burden than the man. For instance, it normally takes nine months to grow and nurse a child internally. Needless to say, it is not an easy job to feed and carry around someone inside your body day and night for nine months. After this long period, this young person is delivered painfully into the world by the mother to see other people and enjoy the blue sky. Yet this guy still needs further attention for a long time before he can be left alone to care for himself. So the duty of the mother to look after him does not end until this little guy grows to know the difference between what is right and what is wrong. Even the young of animals, birds and fish closely attach themselves to their mothers until they grow.

To tell nothing but mere truth, until she leaves this world, a mother never acknowledges that her child has acquired independence—at least not by her attitude towards the child. That is why they are wrongly considered to be meddling in the affairs of their married children's families, even when these children have assumed leadership positions in society. Women always want to see their children excel in life.

Generally, women are kind-hearted; in some way, they see all human beings in the same way they see their own children. This explains why they are always in the forefront, championing the welfare of those who cannot speak for themselves and fighting against those who cause human suffering. Ladies are peace lovers, good administrators and managers, and their analysis of issues leads to great insights. In most cases, a woman will not hesitate to share what they have with others in an effort to improve the latter's quality of life or alleviate their suffering. Above all, women enjoy unique God-given freedom whereby they are not limited by national boundaries and can marry anywhere and start improving the welfare of that place.

Women in our young nation of South Sudan are not an exception in that they have suffered more than men since ancient times. You cannot fathom the mental torture they have had to go through, seeing their children become victims of the exploitation of man by man. Some women have been raped and physically abused by their own sons and foreigners. Some of them have become widows through senseless wars caused by men, while others have lost their children to these wars and left to stare at graves. Many women have suffered so much in their lifetime that they have left this world with less flesh than bones due to hunger and poverty. In the past clashes between communities, women were never involved in the fight. Sadly, this has changed and women are now brutally killed in cold blood by merciless men—their own sons. This is a big shame on us, an abomination in God's eyes and a big challenge to the peaceful co-existence of human beings and a blot on our national image.

In order to improve on our national image, we need to change our attitude towards our women and start loving these dear mothers and sisters and wives as ourselves. They are all God's children in spite of their different socio-economic, political, ethnic and religious backgrounds. It will also greatly benefit society if we respect the skills that our women have and give them equal opportunity with men in the different areas of national development and leadership.

If we men respect our women and love them as ourselves, we will happily coexist and work in our young nation of South Sudan. As a result, people of other nations will respect and love us, and God will bless our land in a big way. In our nation, respect for our women and women from other parts of the world should be diligently promoted, cherished and enforced by our national law. It must be a vital aspect of our national pride.

Respect for the Youth

"Sons are a heritage from the Lord, children a reward from him. Like arrows in the hands of a warrior are sons born in one youth. Blessed is the man whose quiver is full of them. They will not be put to shame when they contend with their enemies in the gate" (Ps.27:3-5).

The above Scripture is evidence of the fact that our Creator blesses us and our children to perpetuate the existence of human beings under the sun. It also shows the importance of our children when it comes to our own security. They are referred to as our crown of pride.

In the new Republic of South Sudan, our children have undergone and are still facing tremendous challenges in life. These challenges include, but not limited to, poor early child care, poor educational system, inadequate girl-child education, child abduction and killing, being orphaned and child labour. Most of our children, especially in rural areas, grow up without an education. This lack of basic education means they cannot acquire important skills and are accordingly unfit for good job opportunities. They have no choice but to join the armed forces and serve in the lower cadre or become casual workers, only earning enough to scrape by. When the going gets too tough, some end up being involved in dirty jobs and bad moral behaviour such as prostitution, heavy drinking, drug consumption, idleness, gossiping and rumour-mongering, theft, cattle rustling, name it. Others give up making any effort to improve their lives and become street families.

The Republic of South Sudan inherited these problems from the old Sudan, although our communities too seemed to promote these same conditions. But we need to face up to the issue and act decisively before things go out of control.

We know that our children are the ones to replace us when we leave this world. If our children are properly taken care of, they will have good moral values, and when they take over from us, they will make up a good society. But if our children are left to go through unfavourable challenges as they grow up, these challenges will have some bad moral impact on their individual behaviour. This does not bode well for a nation that seeks to promote good citizenry.

Now the right questions to ask ourselves are: What kind of South Sudan do we want tomorrow? Do we want a nation that is known for good moral values or poor moral values? If we want a nation with admirable moral values, then it is incumbent on us to seek ways of mentoring our youths so as to prepare them to be the kind of citizens we want them to be. This is a serious project that will require input right from the family level and through school. The government too should craft policies that demonstrate its concern, love and respect for the youth, determined to realize the dream of a dignified South Sudan where there will be no so-called street children. Drawing from the wisdom of God's Word, we should not exasperate our children but bring them up in the love of God to be responsible and respectful citizens of our nation. Respect for the youth should be one of the main goals to diligently work at as a nation.

Respect for the Armed Forces

I wrote this section of the book peacefully seated in a house in Nairobi, Kenya, on 25 June 2014. This peace is as a result of the various security personnel, sacrificing their sleep to ensure security of individuals within the nation's boundaries. These people do not regularly stay with their families in order that other citizens enjoy a good time with their families. Similarly in South Sudan, our national boundaries are secured through the sacrifice of people who have chosen to take it upon themselves to ensure our safety inside the country and to make sure our national boundaries are not violated. Our streets, homes, shops, cinemas and casinos, bars and restaurants, schools and offices, rivers and airports, sports fields, tourist sites, banks and other business places are safe because we have patriotic men and women who love their nation and other citizens more than their own lives. Our national laws are protected and enforced by these respectable national guards.

It is our collective responsibility, together with our government, to ensure that our national guards, whether the military, the police, the prison wardens, those who take care of the wildlife, customs and immigrations officers and other security agencies are taken care of. Let our nation be known worldwide for our people's respect for their own armed forces.

While it is their national duty to guard our nation, it is our obligation as a people to honour their role, love and respect them as our own brothers and sisters. Respect for our armed forces and other security agencies should be one of the signs of our self-esteem as a nation.

Respect for Orphans, Widows, Widowers and Single Ladies

In the eyes of God, orphans, widows and widowers and single mothers are as important as any other human beings. In most cases, people do not find themselves in such circumstances of their own choice. Hence, they deserve kindness, love and respect like the people who are in favourable circumstances.

The bitter war of independence did bequeath the Republic of South Sudan a huge number of orphans, widows and widowers and single mothers. Parents were killed and left their children behind; husbands died and left their wives; wives died and left their husbands and children, and some ladies were sexually violated by uncaring, dehumanising men and left to take care of their unfortunate babies singlehandedly. Of course, there is no single nation in the world that is without such unfortunate people, even without such wars.

Some of these disadvantaged people are our own brothers and sisters. In order for them to enjoy life as respected citizens, it is our moral duty and that of our people's government to do to them the follow things.

First, it is the duty of the people's government and other child-caring actors to establish and manage major orphanages in the country to look after our orphans, especially those who have lost both parents. The orphanages should be complete outfits that include both formal and vocational schools. Children should be domiciled there until they reach the age of maturity. That would be the sure way of preventing them from becoming street children or urchins. But strict regulations are necessary to guard this huge project against being misused by selfish exploiters.

Second, legislation should be put in place to protect the possessions and personal integrity of individuals belonging in these vulnerable groups of people from possible violators. These people are entitled to equal opportunities just like other citizens within the country.

Third, we should love and respect our orphans, widows, widowers and single women just like any other citizens and with the same intensity as we love ourselves. This should be one of the admirable causes of our national pride.

Respect for National Resources

For our discussion in this book, I have decided to divide national wealth into two: private and public wealth. Private wealth is the one owned either by individual or a group of individuals. It may constitute resources emanating from a family's business venture that is owned and managed by group of people. This wealth directly or indirectly benefits the entire nation through a variety of ways such as providing employment, revenue to the government in form of tax, and tangible and intangible services. National development is always a joint venture by the government and private sectors. Moreover, the nation benefits even from investments made by foreigners.

Private property should be appreciated and respected by all South Sudanese people, especially if it is honestly acquired. We should cultivate the noble spirit of being happy with those who are happy and being sad with those who are sad. This brotherly spirit of respect for private property will promote national cohesion and entrepreneurial effort and provide a conducive business environment for private and foreign investments.

It is very unfortunate that some greedy, selfish people consider public wealth as nobody's wealth, not even common wealth. Such are they who view the government as an entity that is detached from people. They compare it to an old, wealthy and childless man with no one to inherit or protect his property, and therefore, his wealth can be looted without fearing any penalty. This explains why there is widespread misuse of public resources by people whose conscience seems to have been seared.

But the fact of the matter is that public resources are acquired and managed by the government for the common good of all citizens. This wealth consists of different types of assets. Using these resources, the government is able to render services (some of which only it can provide) like health, education, road building and maintenance, communication systems and national security, among others. Public resources belong to all the people of the land. They do not belong to one person, not even to the people's leader or a certain group of influential people; they are for the benefit of all.

When some government officials try to divert some government resources to their private use, they do so in violation of people's rights. This is stealing people's wealth, a selfish, criminal act, which is punishable by the national law in part of the world. Public wealth must not be mistaken for private wealth; the former is intended for the common benefit of all the people of the land. There are many adverse results of the widespread misuse of public wealth.

First, the looters of public resources become richer and richer while their fellow countrymen become poorer and poorer. This automatically leads to antagonism and disunity as the gap between the haves and have not widens.

Second, the misuse of public resources creates disparities in the kind of houses people live in. The affluent dwell in stately mansions, whereas the rest of the people live in rickety shacks in sprawling shanties that lack basic amenities. The result is a nation that lacks cohesiveness because one group feels defrauded.

Third, the poor majority end up as servants of the few rich. In a nation where a few of her people live way above the poverty line while the rest of the people languish in poverty will not be a peaceful country; it is a nation where man is eating man and hence, man hates man. Such a nation will be full of crime and will ultimately attract a curse from God.

In relation to our national wealth, how do we handle our national wealth? We ought to respect and protect our national wealth and manage it for the common good of all if we really cherish and uphold our national moral principles of justice for all, liberty for all, prosperity for all, equality for all, fear and love of God and love for one another.

This will make our young nation of South Sudan a prosperous nation where every man feels at home and loves and respects fellow countrymen. That is how we will build a nation where God feels at home and a nation that is loved and respected by others. So respect for national wealth should be one of the foundations of our national pride.

The Importance of Self-Respect

When God's Word exhorts us to love others as we love ourselves, he wants us to truly love ourselves first before we extend the same love to our neighbours. If you don't love and respect yourself, you are not positioned to love and respect others. When you love and respect yourself, you will ensure that you match your deeds, words and thoughts with your self-image. Moreover, people love and respect you with the same measure by which you love and respect yourself. Love and respect are earned and bestowed; they are not demanded.

The moment you lose self-respect, other human beings will automatically withdraw their respect from you. Even God Himself will not respect you, although he may continue loving you and be ready to deepen His relationship with you if you change.

The behaviour of man is basically the same worldwide, irrespective of one's colour of skin and socio-economic, geopolitical, religious and cultural status. Man is made in God's own image and likeness. But it takes valuing himself as a child of God if he is to enjoy the benefits that his Maker has given him and walk with his head high in the realm of mankind.

Yet man could have a low opinion of himself despite his position in God's creation due to his physical appearance and his environment. As a result, he may start to exhibit low self-esteem, lending his back for others to walk over. As a result, he begins to view himself as nobody while regarding everyone else as somebody.

Today in South Sudan, some people have lost their self-esteem following protracted periods of social, economic and political oppression. The result has been a mental slavery that makes them lose faith in themselves as human beings, entertaining the impression that they are nothing, have nothing to offer to society and can do nothing by themselves. This attitude even makes them not to love, appreciate or respect their own body make-up, including their beautiful skin colour. And not just that, they consider foreign workers more important than local experts, even where locals have skills that match those of foreigners.

This is evident from the way in which some unskilled and inexperienced foreigners have been given key jobs in the private and public sector, thus, raking in vast amounts of our national wealth in form of salaries. One of these days try to visit a government office in the company of a foreigner, and you will be shocked at the amount of respect he will be accorded compared to you. Yet my experience whenever I have travelled overseas has been different: there they respect their nationals more than foreigners. They value their own more than others and depend more on each other.

Really, South Sudan is a blessed nation in terms of skilled manpower. Thousands of our sons and daughters hold respected qualifications—diploma, certificates, bachelor, master and PhD degrees from recognised universities in all sorts of countries like USA, Canada, Australia and UK. This is not to mention many others in institutions of higher learning in Kenya, Uganda and Ethiopia, among others. Were we to invite these intellectuals to return home to help with the building of our national foundation, the current talk of lack of skilled manpower would cease. Better still, these people would earn their money and invest it locally to benefit our economy.

Another unedifying example is how our people prefer business deals with foreigners instead of their fellow countrymen. Such deals include banking and money transfers, and they are unaware that in most cases they are taken advantage of. But every time such people will come up with lame excuses in support of not dealing with local businessmen and women.

Some of these arguments include: locals sell their things expensively; they are not polite; theirs are low quality goods. What such people do not understand is that they are destroying their own country's economy and building foreign ones instead. By buying from foreigners we inadvertently ensure that they are always in business; yet they plough back the money we pay them to strengthen their nations' economies. Then they buy and bring more goods to South Sudan and the exploitation continues. Knowingly or unknowingly, we become mere consumers of foreign goods and expertise, building other economies at the expense of ours.

Whether they produce low quality or high quality goods, our infant industries deserve our collective backing because this will prove to be in the interest of our own nation in the long run. If you don't appreciate what is yours, who will?

I do not mean to be selfish by reasoning the way I do. I am

merely advising my gullible compatriots to always remember, whenever they are faced with a business deal, that they have their own country to build. That way they will approach such deals wisely. And I believe that I am being objective in asking my people to be cautious. A key evidence of self-esteem is to respect and value what one makes more than what their neighbour makes.

Another negative result of low self-esteem is the manner in which we portray ourselves and our nation in the foreigners' eyes. But what we should know is that there is no single person or group of people or a nation that is perfect under the sun. I have problems; you have problems. All of us as human beings have flaws. Even the First World nations and the revered leaders (including church leaders) of the world have their weak points which they are quietly and constantly working at daily. What matters is the way in which one deals with their flaws. Exposing your weaknesses to unconcerned outsiders is a sign of defeat and low self-esteem.

But the worst thing that I have come to know about us is the way we talk ill of ourselves and our nation in the eyes of others. We speak ill concerning our national leaders, our government, our churches, our nation and one another as if we are the worst and most disadvantaged people on earth. Do you believe that those whom we constantly feed with wrong impressions about us and our nation care, or are willing to respect us? No way, they will despise all of us plus our nation. A family where the husband and wife and their children talk ill of one another and share their problems with anyone they meet in the streets is the worst family under the sun.

What do we do to project ourselves, our nation and our locally produced things as valuable? If we acted on the answer to this question, South Sudan would immediately become a respected young nation with a dignified people in the community of nations. Yet I will not answer this question alone. The answer calls for the participation of all the South Sudanese people, males and females, young and old, poor and rich. Everyone must take the question as a crucial national assignment if we really want to regain our lost self-esteem. But allow me to highlight a few relevant points.

First, building our national self-esteem calls for a programme that involves all sections of our society and made to inform all public and private activities. For instance, these include our national games, sports, art and music, among others.

Second, we should value one another as human beings, including our leaders, despite their weaknesses as individuals. We should also value our locally manufactured products. We should value our traditional foods. We must respect our folklore and the words of wisdom handed down by our forefathers. We should value the skills of our people and desire to exploit them by giving them work. We should appreciate and support all our games, sports, art and music. We should appreciate our separate and collective strengths. We should appreciate our diversity when it comes to different ethnic groups and their unique languages and cultures. We should appreciate and support our local business enterprises and business ideas originated by locals. We should cherish, uphold and safeguard our national image. In short, we should value and support our people and everything about us, by us, of us and for us without feeling guilty because there is nothing racist or selfish about this. If I want to live in my house happily until I leave this world, experience shows that I would have to love it more than anyone else's house.

If we embrace a healthy love and healthy respect for ourselves, for our things and for our nation, we will have a healthy love and healthy respect for other people and their things or their nations. Accordingly, they will have healthy love and healthy respect for us and our things and our nation.

In our young nation of South Sudan, we should first embrace self-respect if we are to expect other people to respect us. This noble principle should be pursued, embraced and safeguarded by all of us and made one of the foundations if we are to build our nation's image.

Respect for Aliens

In the common sense of the word, 'alien' means foreigner or stranger. The word refers to a person who is in a foreign land legally or illegally. There are many legal reasons that allow a foreigner to enter into, stay and work in a foreign nation. He may be there as a refugee, or on a work or resident or student permit. One may be a private or official visitor on a short visit and hence, holding a legitimate national visa. One could also be an employee working in their national embassy in a foreign country. An alien may be someone given a political asylum. These are some of the reasons that make one to be in a foreign land. Anyone in a foreign land for different reasons may be termed as an unlawful visitor. If conditions for repatriation are not easy, such a person will languish in a foreign jail or be confined to a specific place for quite some time until his case is finally determined.

In every country, there are international and national laws that govern the status of any category of foreigner. For example, the status of a refugee is different from the status of one with a work permit or one with a temporary visitor visa. Only those with official work permits are entitled to do some specific jobs in a foreign nation, and these permits have a time limit.

While in a foreign land, one is required to strictly comply with the laws of the host nation. If he violates any of them, he will be dealt with accordingly. He may be arrested, imprisoned or sent back to his country of origin. Every foreigner is to respect himself and respect his host country.

Most people are likely to find themselves in a foreign country at one time or the other. And since an alien is just a human being like any of us, he deserves love, respect and humane treatment from other people. Even if he violates the laws of his host country, he merits access to justice like the citizens.

As I write this book, we have a huge number of foreigners in the Republic of South Sudan. Very few of them are in the country legally as either authentic refugees, genuine employees of foreign embassies, holders of legal work permit, esteemed temporary visitors, holders of legal resident permits or political asylum seekers. Most foreigners qualify as unlawful aliens. But though they may be in South Sudan illegally, they are not to blame because they did not just drop there from the sky. They were allowed to enter the country by some of our national guards to work and live within our boundaries. Thus, it is our national and moral obligation to love and respect them as human beings, too.

But even if the section of our law that deals with foreigners were invoked to deal with these illegal foreigners, it would still better be dealt with within the legal framework, providing that the international law is not flouted in the process. No South Sudanese citizen is allowed to take the law into his own hands to mistreat any foreigner, irrespective of his legal status. In addition, even if there were to be any diplomatic differences between South Sudan and another country, this would not justify disrespecting the embassy of such a country or her nationals who work in our country.

We and our nation of South Sudan should be law-abiding, a people known for respecting foreigners who are within our national borders. Our respect for aliens and their possessions should be one of our national moral values.

Respect for and Obedience to the Law

Human beings have been rebellious by nature since the fall of Adam and Eve in the Garden of Eden. That is why God decreed laws governing their conduct, including the familiar Ten Commandments, to govern the relationship between God and man on one hand and man and man on the other. Laws are not meant to harm people or serve as a hindrance; if anything, they are there to safeguard and promote people's personal and collective aspirations so as to make their living and working environments friendly and peaceful.

Since laws are made by people and for the people, then it is imperative that the people respect and obey their own laws. When the national law safeguards people's interests, then people will respect and obey it and vice versa.

In the young Republic of South Sudan, part of our obligation as a nation is to make and implement laws that protect people and their property and guide their conduct as they pursue their aspirations, in their relationships, as they do their jobs, etc. In addition, our laws should safeguard, promote and enhance our national image.

Our national law should be a respecter of no persons apart from itself. That way it will have proven impartial and hence, deserving our unequivocal support. We should aspire for impartial courts of law where we can shame and discipline our own rebellious people without the need to take them outside the country to stand before external courts like the ICC for trial. We ought to prove a sovereign nation in every way, including having a respectable judicial system.

As a people, we should aspire for genuine respect for our national law. Even if we felt like our national law is unfriendly, we should still respect and obey it as we seek to have it amended so as to become friendly and one that serves our interests and those of our visitors.

Respect for Politics and the Government

A government of the few, by the few and for the few can only be loved and respected by the few because it is there to satisfy narrow private interests. But a government of the people, by the people and for the people is loved and respected by all the people, for it champions individual and collective aspirations. People love and respect their own government if it loves and respects them in return. Moreover, a people's government comes with collective ownership and responsibility.

In the Republic of South Sudan, the popular government is the people's government, which is put in place and ran by people's representatives. Basically, it consists of the executive, the legislature and the judiciary. These three branches of government are supposed to cooperate by harmonising and coordinating their activities in order to deliver vital services to all the people. The government should be the people's servant.

Whether people in South Sudan are satisfied with their government now is hard to tell. But even if they are not happy with it, whose responsibility is it to make them happy with it? Since it is a people's government, it is the sole responsibility of the people themselves to mould it, own and make it relevant in taking care of their varied interests. A government is nothing but people, so South Sudanese make up the government of South Sudan.

No one else has the capacity to make your government morally good or bad; citizens have the inalienable moral responsibility to either make theirs a good government and praise themselves for the work well-done or make it terribly bad and blame themselves for work poorly done. So people should not stand afar and criticise their own government as if it is a foreign entity.

If people are not pleased with their government, it is their duty to look for ways of reforming it peacefully for the common good of all. Government officials should not oppose people's desire to make changes within their own government. But if the officials have genuine reasons behind their opposing such proposals, it is their national right to express them to other citizens lovingly and convincingly. People should avoid wrangles that would destroy their government and lead to insecurity. They should be mature enough to know how to lovingly find local solutions to their problems; imported solutions for local issues have never succeeded.

All in all, since the government is nothing but the people themselves, the South Sudanese citizens have a moral obligation to love and respect their own government. If we love and respect our government, others will love and respect it and love us, too. Promoting people's love and respect for their own government should be mainstreamed as one of the ways of enhancing our national self-esteem.

'Politics' has different meanings, but in this book, it refers to a group of people who seek to influence the way a nation is governed. And the default way by which politicians market themselves is by promising to manage the affairs of the nation in a better way so as to offer better services and champion the aspirations of citizens. Such pledges include economic growth, expansion of democratic space, improved educational system and better health services, improved national security, equal access to justice, gender equality, mainstreaming youth and child welfare, increased job opportunities, better social security, among others. All politicians like to portray themselves as having the interests of the people of their nation at heart.

But good politicking is not just mere rhetoric, a game played by the witty, rich and well-educated who are endowed with a gift of the gab. It is not even for those who want to quickly enrich themselves at the expense of the very people they claim to want to help. Good politicking is a sacrificial but noble work done wisely by people with high integrity for the welfare of the people of their nation.

Hence, it is the moral and national obligation of all the citizens of South Sudan to see to it that they always appoint to political office people who have completely submerged their self-interests in the sea of their people's aspirations. Politics should be allowed to unite rather than divide us; it should be a blessing, not a curse. Our nation ought to be a shining star in the field of global politics.

Sharing the National Cake

Unfair sharing of food is the root cause of most forms of human conflict in this world. But since many cultures consider fighting over food as demeaning and an expression of glutton, it is often glossed over, with people citing other seemingly more honourable reasons as the cause of the strife. These reasons may include bad politics, poor administration, religious differences, racialism, geography, marginalisation, etc. Fighting over food is common in the family setting, among teams of people, within and between two communities, within a nation, between two countries and even between God and man as it happened in the Garden of Eden. Even when you see animals fighting, it is often for survival as they fight over water and grazing sources. Some even kill each other over food. In other words, when you see and hear people fighting over territories, water and grazing sources, they are really fighting over food; it is a war of the stomach.

When food is not equally shared among people, people quarrel and fight among themselves. But if they employ the principle of sharing food equally among people, they will arrive at a compromise, reconcile and live together as brothers and sisters in the same geographical location. Other times people take their share of resources and depart to go and use it in isolation. This can occur even among the sons and daughters of the same parents. If the people who have been into small groups again sense inequality in the sharing of food, they will fight among themselves and split further. And this goes on and on. Actually the result of inequality in the sharing of food is what has fuelled the splitting up of communities from time immemorial.

While people are fighting over food and breaking up into small groups, normally the stronger person always takes the lion's share and hence, incurs the wrath of the weak, although such may be pent up wrath. Thereafter, the strong person clings to his big share, ready to protect it at whatever cost. Meanwhile, the brain of the weak person goes into overdrive as he develops strategies of getting his food share that the strong has deprived him of using any means possible. This has been the cause of family and community feuds and even regional and international wars.

At the time of my writing, the young Republic of South

Sudan is being governed using decentralisation system. Starting from the lowest unit of governance we have buma, payam, county and then national government. Dividing the nation into small administrative units is necessitated for effective governance that is characterised by the availing of services to all the people.

But as if this system has been unable to deliver services, some people are now asking for the introduction of federal government system, a very expensive system even for nations endowed with much more resources. I remember clearly the proposal for a federal system of government was informally made sometime in 2012 in Equatoria Region. The reason given for it was that there was an unfair distribution of customs and immigration revenue, especially between Central and Eastern Equatoria States on one hand and the National Government in Juba on the other hand. These funds were mostly collected along the South Sudan-Kenya border and South Sudan-Uganda border, and that is why the two states featured prominently.

But even if federalism were to be adopted, I believe that would not automatically translate into fair distribution of the national cake, and the same dissatisfied people will call for confederacy. I wonder what they will call for if that system of government does not work.

Some people believe that decentralisation is the ultimate solution when it comes to equitable distribution of the national cake. But I hold a different view. For instance, if this cake were to be fairly divided to the complete satisfaction of all citizens, they will live harmoniously even under a centralised system of government. Thus, if we want to maintain our territorial cohesion, it is incumbent on us and our government to explore ways of sharing our vast national resources as fairly as possible.

We can learn a lot from the functioning of the human

body. For one to be whole, every single part of the body receives constant supply of blood from the heart. This highly coordinated system is a marvel. The moment the blood fails to reach a certain part of the body, even the smallest part, the whole body suffers. This is so because different parts need each other for the entire body to maintain its healthy appearance and work efficiently and effectively. The big and small, strong and weak parts are equally important in the body.

Just like the human body, all parts of our nation should receive requisite attention. And for cohesion and peaceful coexistence among our people, the distribution of our resources among the sons and daughters of the land should be done as efficiently as blood circulating in the human body. Each part of our nation, be it big or small, strong or weak, should receive its fair share of 'blood'. Let us all enjoy or suffer together in love.

Fair distribution of the national cake should be one of the important principles upon which our young nation of South Sudan is founded. This of course, is in keeping with justice for all, liberty for all, prosperity for all, equality for all, fear and love of God and our love for one another. People who eat together live together happily. Do not let food be the one to destroy our brotherly love and fragment our beautiful nation.

Tolerance and Forgiveness

When people stay together, even for a short period of time, they are likely to offend each other, unknowingly or sometimes intentionally. Our words and deeds also sometimes injure the feelings of others. This could occur at the family setting, at business places, at social gatherings, along the streets, in the political arena, in government offices and even within the four corners of the house of God. There is no one who has never injured someone else's feelings. People often hurt their beloved wives, husbands or children, making them restless and sleepless. You and I have some enemies, and we too are regarded as enemies by other people.

There are many ways by which human beings make enemies among themselves, but I can only mention a few of them here. First, people can feel justified to hate each other due to mistakes done to each other, whether intentionally or unintentionally. Second, people may hate each other because of past mistakes done by them or by their forefathers. Third, people may hate you, not because of anything wrong you have done to them but simply because they don't like your good character. This of course, is prompted by jealousy and ignorance. Fourth, some people may hate others with no reason at all. In such cases, when you ask the hater why he hates so and so, the common answer is, "I can't tell, but I don't like him anyway. Maybe my blood and his do not mix." But must the blood of people mix for them to love each other, and if so, who does the mixing?

One thing that I have discovered in life is that some people are experts in making enemies, and they do this deliberately. Such people will move around interacting with people but focus on other people's flaws, no matter how insignificant, to justify their hatred of them. And as they move around weighed down by their baskets of hatred on their tired heads, they keep saying, "So and so is a bad person. He said or has done this and that to me. I will surely pay him back dearly with what he will never forget." Such people boast of having an endless list of so-called enemies. These kinds of people are never happy unless they make others unhappy.

And our world is not short of such people. For instance, when Jesus Christ came into this world, being God but condescending to take human form to work out salvation in his life and bring us the Good News, you might think He would be loved by everybody. But it was the very people that He intended to save that humiliated and brutally crucified him. Similarly, we too have people in our midst who enjoy making our lives and those of our families uncomfortable and others who make our communities and nations uncomfortable. But such people deserve our forgiveness and also God's forgiveness, because as Jesus said concerning those who crucified Him: 'Father, forgive them, for they do not know what they are doing' (Lk.23:34a).

Aware of the sinfulness of man's heart and hence, the importance of unmerited forgiveness, our Lord in the book of Matthew 6:43-48 admonishes us not to love our good neighbours and hate our enemies. He instructs us to love our enemies also and pray for those who persecute us. Jesus knows that when hatred is met with hatred, it gives birth to even more intense and hence, dangerous hatred, the kind of hatred that will eventually drown mankind and other creatures alive. Moreover, Jesus knows more than anyone else that the best drugs for the treatment of hatred are love and forgiveness.

As I write, previously beautiful houses in South Sudan have been reduced to rubble, with their furniture and other possessions looted. Precious human blood is being recklessly poured due to reckless skirmishes. National orphanages are inundated with children who are losing parents daily. The number of widows, widowers and crippled people is increasing daily at an obscene rate. Feeling threatened, some innocent citizens have had to abandon their homes and seek refuge elsewhere in and outside their own nation, sometimes living in undignified and unsanitary dwellings. Arable lands and fertile farms are lying fallow as food prices skyrocket. Our beloved sons and daughters are having to contend with extreme heat and sometimes cold, hunger and thirst while hiding in unhealthy trenches and fox holes. The flow of our national oil has been interrupted. Our esteemed local and foreign investors are now reconsidering their decisions as certain foreigners and locals who are driven by greed are exploiting the sad situation of insecurity to enrich themselves while denting our national image. The love for God and the love for one another has greatly waned as the spirit of hatred takes over. The raping of our dear sisters, wives and mothers by their own dehumanised and godless sons, brothers and husbands has become the order of the day, leaving them in terrible shame. The list of undesirable consequences of our wrongdoing, hatred, jealousy and selfishness is quite endless. In many ways we are regressing as individuals and as a nation.

But why are we in such a horrible mess? The answer: We have lost the noble spirit of tolerance and forgiveness. If we were to follow our moral principles—justice for all, liberty for all, prosperity for all, equality for all, fear and love of God as well as love for one another—we would have avoided this nationwide mess.

Yet wise people say: Better late than never. The best thing in life is not how to avoid making or entering into a problem; the best thing in life, however, is how to come out of it and try not to repeat it.

As I write, I have very high hope that with God's help, we will come out of this mess and avoid making the same mistake in future, especially if we will embrace, cherish, internalise and apply the noble principles of tolerance and forgiveness.

If we strive to tolerate and forgive one another, we will live in peace in our nation. There will be unity and prosperity for all. All our good and bad leaders will be working, living and dying peacefully at home. Other nations will tolerate and forgive any mistakes we have done. But not just that, our loving, compassionate God too will forgive our personal and collective sins and bless us. Let's be mature and loving enough to tolerate and forgive one another.

Religious Tolerance

Human beings are religious by nature, since there is a void in the heart of man that only God can fill. Unfortunately, the devil takes advantage of this and proffers all sorts of idols to people to worship. Some of the major religions in the world are Christianity, Islam, Buddhism and Hinduism. In Africa, we have a host of religious sects that are categorized as ATRs (African Traditional Religions).

Since time immemorial, religion has been accused of being the major cause of sectarian violence. That is why people cringe at the mention of Christian Crusade or Islamic Jihad. But the right question to ask ourselves is whether religion is really the one to blame for the past and today's human sufferings that has now taken global proportions. Personally, I believe our inherited Adamic nature is the real cause of the problems that face humanity.

Even before the advent of Christianity and Islam, human beings were still practising some forms of religion as a way of dealing with their challenges. In the course of that, religion may have regrettably come to be part of their problems rather than a solution. We would be mistaken, however, to blame religion for our chronic problems. Really, man himself is the true source of his own problem. Indeed, even in the so-called socialist or communist countries where religion is silenced, problems still exist—more problems than those in places where religion is left to thrive.

But what I see as the problem is people wanting to use religion to achieve their own selfish interests as a result of which they are forced to change its teachings to accommodate their selfish objectives. For really, if the aim of a religion is to worship God, the Creator of heaven and earth, why would worshipers hate and seek to destroy each other? Even those who ignorantly mistake God for graven images and pay their allegiance to them, why should they hate fellow worshippers of the same images and other human beings in the name of religion?

But putting religion aside, if people were to act humanely among themselves, they would protect each other from the day-to-day challenges and make it possible to live comfortably and peacefully in this world. Hence, the main source of human problems, according to me, is not religion but the dangerous erosion of moral values. Man has learned to use religion as a silent scapegoat to justify the undesirable results of his sinful nature. Religion has never ever been the problem; depraved man hiding behind religion as he clings to his selfishness is the problem.

There are different Christian denominations in South Sudan, all of which preach the crucified Christ and worship the same God of the Bible. They are the branches of the same Vine, Jesus Christ, according to the gospel of John 15:1-8. And from our experience with trees, we know that the branches of a tree love each other; they take equal share of the same food items, sunlight and air, and they live in peace and protect each other, especially in the case of harsh weather. The braches enhance the beauty of the tree.

Elsewhere in the Bible, Jesus commands his followers to love one another, just as he loves them, so that other people know that they are his disciples. Apostle John corroborates that message as follows:

> "We love because he first loved us. If anyone says, 'I love God,' yet hates his brother, he is a liar. For anyone who does not love his brother, whom he has seen, cannot love God, whom he has not seen. And he has given us this command: whoever loves God must also love his brother" (1 Jn.4:19-21).

The undeniable truth is that we cannot claim to love God with all the heart, mind and soul without loving our neighbours as ourselves. Our sincere love of God, whom we have not physically seen, compels us to love our fellow brothers and sisters with whom we physically interact daily. If we don't love our fellow human beings, we will be hypocritical in claiming to love God.

You and I are entitled to our conclusion whether Christians really cherish and manage to live by these noble principles. And if they don't obey and live by this great commandment, then which commandments of our Lord and Saviour Jesus Christ do they obey? Besides, how will non-Christians know that they are real disciples of Jesus Christ if they don't love one another?

As followers of the same God, religion should unite us rather than separate us. Instead, we are to love one another, work and live together in harmony in the nation of South Sudan. We should also appreciate the areas in which we agree so far as religious teachings are concerned and be ready to be tolerant when it comes to religious teachings in which we differ. Moreover, people should be free to teach what they believe so long as they are not forcing their beliefs on others.

Our young nation should be a safe haven where people of different religious persuasions live harmoniously.

Any religion that brings more harm than good to our people should be roundly condemned and rejected. The Creator of heaven and earth and all the things therein lovingly says, "For I know the plans I have for you....plans to prosper you and not to harm you, plans to give you hope and a future' (Jer.29:11). So any religious teaching that propagates plans to harm and deny us hope and a future has its origin with Satan whom the Bible calls the thief. This is because "The thief comes only to steal and kill and destroy" (John 10:10). This kind of harmful religion must not benefit from our generousity when it comes to freedom of worship.

For the people of South Sudan to reap the benefits of religious variations and tolerance, all religions should aim at promoting justice for all, liberty for all, prosperity for all, equality for all, fear and love of God as well as our genuine love for one another. If we really worship one God, I believe he would be pleased to have his children exercise their different faiths harmoniously. Concerning matters of the spirit, we should strive for unity and harmony in diversity.

Good Neighbourliness

No man is an island, so sang a famous musician of the '60s. In the same way, no nation is self-contained in everything as to exist without needing other nations. Even the earth is a part of the universe. That is how we are able to benefit from moonshine and sunshine that comes from other celestial bodies in the solar system. Accordingly, we need each other, and our nations badly need each other, since in today's world, our economics, geopolitics, culture, etc. are very much intertwined. This is to say that your problem is my problem, and my problem is your problem. For example, we are now faced with global warming, a problem that affects even those of us who never participated in damaging the ozone layer. It is therefore, our collective responsibility as human beings to initiate or improve on and safeguard our existing national, regional and international relationships so as to make each and every part of our world safe for living by people and conducive for the existence of other creatures.

How Our Young Nation Should Conduct Herself

What should our newly established nation of South Sudan do to have a respectable place in the community of world nations? This question might have been answered directly or indirectly within our national constitution and other relevant official policy documents. But I would love to add my voice here as one of the national citizens.

As I project my mental vision into thousands of years to come, if Jesus delays his second coming, I would love to see a neutral Republic of South Sudan which is living harmoniously with her neighbours and other nations of the world, irrespective of their socio-economic and political status. I have many reasons in support of this view, but within the limit of this book, I would like to highlight just a few.

The Dinka have the saying that a child belongs to all people. Babies are innocent little creatures that are peaceful and easily respond to love. They see all people as loving, lovable and compassionate. While they do not have real enemies, they regard a multitude of people as real friends. They are neutral when it comes to whom to side with. That is why they are easily adaptable and adoptable. To illustrate the neutrality of a child, when there is a fight between adults, and especially between its own parents, the child does not take sides. Eager to see peace restored but unable to separate the two 'warriors', the child merely cries in an effort to call those who have what it takes to rescue the situation. A child does not meddle in other people's affairs. As a result, its neutrality influences adults to leave children unharmed whenever families or communities are fighting, although this humane attitude is changing in certain cultures. Conscientious adults do not even dare to defraud children of what is rightfully theirs. They view them as too innocent and helpless to steal from.

It has been said that in Africa, it takes the whole village to raise a child, although this truism could be global as well. Accordingly, borrowing from the example of the life of a child, it would be wise for our young nation to assume a neutral position in the community of nations. As a young nation, South Sudan needs the wisdom of governance and other forms of assistance that different countries in the globe have to offer so as to be effectively nurtured to the level of political and socio-economic maturity.

True, there are children who are very aggressive by nature. In spite of their young age, they keep rebelling against their parents' and other adults' requirements. In their naiveté, their ego deceives them that they can compete with the adults and win, so they start acting like adults and requiring the respect that goes with adulthood. But before long, their parents and other adults ran out of patience and mercilessly deal with these stubborn children. No wonder such children lead a difficult life and end up with scars of lacerations all over the body. They also grow hating people because of the beatings they receive as they grow. Finding themselves in the ocean of poverty and lacking an education, some of them resort to all sorts of criminal behaviour.

If, in dealing with other nations, our young nation were to emulate the behaviour of an aggressive, stubborn child, her end would be similar: regrets. As the youngest republic both in Africa and the entire world, our young nation should refrain from meddling in the affairs of other nations, even if it is enticed to do so. We should genuinely love all the other nations, whether we agree with the ideologies that guide their governments or not, and seek to live in peace with them. For our country to have a healthy foundation, it should sincerely seek to be a peace-loving nation that enjoys good relationship with the other countries of the world.

How the Faiths Should Relate in South Sudan

First of all, it is important to start by mentioning that religious plurality is enshrined in the constitution of South Sudan. Of the major religions, Christianity has the largest number of followers, followed by Islam and then the ATRs. When it comes to Christianity and Islam, our nation occupies an important point in that it is the bridge that connects the Christians of the northern and eastern part of Africa and also a bridge that connects the Muslims of the northern and eastern parts of Africa. It is therefore, our role to diligently and impartially guard this religious bridge for the common good of mankind and unity and peace in our continent of Africa. This of course, cannot be fully realized without adopting the policy of neutrality in South Sudan.

There has never been a home-grown religious problem in South Sudan; so far the followers of different faiths have been co-existing peacefully. Sometimes they even intermarry. Christians and Muslims invite each other and enjoy together during the time they are celebrating their religious feasts.

One day in May or June 2014, I heard the Secretary General

of the South Sudan Islamic Council Mr. Thahir Bior Lueth Ajak on the national radio, saying that the proposed Islamic university would accept all interested students, irrespective of their religious backgrounds. It seems the aim of this university is to provide quality education to our people, not necessarily to convert them to Islam, although there is nothing bad if a non-Muslim student converts to Islam of his own volition. The faith one chooses to follow is a personal choice. The statement by the General Secretary is no doubt a sign of the peaceful co-existence of South Sudanese who belong to the different religious faiths, a state of affairs that we would want to promote for the common good of our nation and her people.

We should continue promoting healthy religious pluralism and good neighbourliness with the other nations and make it clear that we are never in favour of any kind of religious war.

Thus, we must have good relationships with all African nations, all Arab countries, Israel, European nations, Canada, USA, Caribbean Islands, Latin American nations, Australia, New Zealand and Asian nations. Religion must not divide but unite us as a people.

The Boundaries of South Sudan

The Republic of South Sudan has a respectable place in the region despite being landlocked. Our country borders Sudan, the Central Africa Republic, the Democratic Republic of the Congo, Uganda, Kenya and Ethiopia. These nations have very strong ties with us as explained below.

South Sudan-Sudan border: This is the longest border, though there are disputes concerning it that are yet to be settled as well as the determination of the status of Abyei. Concerning cultures, the two countries share a lot as the two states were one nation until 2011. Although South Sudan separated from Sudan after decades of a long bloody war, our people should not regard people of Sudan as enemies. This is because family feuds are a normal thing even in other parts of the world. Disputes in the family once resolved should be forgotten, even if they led to the family members separating.

It is important to mention that if there was any dispute between the Southerners and Northerners before we separated, it was decided in Khartoum by a clique of government officers there. The marginalisation of the South by the North was not a policy planned and implemented by all the Northerners. But even if all Northerners had been involved, would that be a good reason for people of an independent nation of South Sudan to continue holding fast to ill feelings towards their brothers and sisters? If separation of the South from Sudan was the primary reason behind the civil wars that were waged, then we should live happily with each other now that the goal was achieved. We should understand that no matter how much a child is mistreated by its unkind parents, he or she will not stop being their child.

As a matter of fact, South Sudan should appreciate the current Khartoum Government under the leadership of President Omar Hassan Al Bashir for encouraging and facilitating a peaceful separation of the South from Sudan. His presence in Juba with his top government officials during the historical declaration as well as his endorsement of the historical Independence of South Sudan and his subsequent visits to Juba and the presence of Sudan Embassy in Juba are laudable gestures and clear signs of Sudan's respect for South Sudan's territorial integrity.

I believe that people of Sudan, on their part, have no ill feelings towards the South Sudanese, despite the delayed determination of the boundary between the two nations and the status of Abyei. There is no way these two nations will enjoy regional cooperation as well as belonging in the same Commonwealth of Nations before forgetting their past hostilities and normalising their relationships. If the two nations became friends, I don't think it would be wise for the young nation of South Sudan to spend the huge amount of money required to get our oil to the seaport at other parts of region for export; we should continue shipping it through Port Sudan instead. Also normalised relations would enable us to reap the benefits of economies of scale.

Without talking for Sudan, it is incumbent on us people of South Sudan to totally discard any ill-feelings that we may be holding towards Sudan and her people and open a fresh page and start promoting peace, love, friendliness and good neighbourliness between us and Sudan. And this would not be too difficult because our two countries have cultural connections. This is evident from the fact that we have a huge number of Sudanese in our country and an equally large number of our own brothers and sisters in Sudan.

Some former colonies fought nasty wars of independence with their colonisers, yet they are now the best of friends despite the fact some do not even share common boundaries. Examples include the US and Britain and Kenya and Britain. For the sake of their common good as well as the general welfare of the region and the entire world, it is wise for South Sudan and Sudan to urgently find amicable solutions to their common problems. They should also join hands and help each other address their problems peacefully. May I reiterate here that it is imperative that the two nations pursue cordial relations! Wise people easily give up their differences for the sake of unity and peaceful co-existence, end result being socio-economic and other benefits for all.

South Sudan-Central Africa Republic border: There has been an enabling relationship between the two nations even before our country became independent. The two nations have cordial racial and religious ties. They have a lot in common; so they are well placed to benefit from each other. It is important that we strengthen our bilateral relations with the Central Africa Republic for the benefit of the region and the entire world. We hope that these friendly nations will keep improving on their good neighbourliness.

South Sudan-Democratic Republic of the Congo border: The two nations are not only connected geographically, but there are ethnic groups that straddle the border as well. There are people in both countries who speak the same language. It is a similar bond that influenced Congo, formerly known as Zaire, to open her doors wide to Southern Sudanese people during the seventeen-year civil war (1955-1972), known as the Anyanya Movement. Southern Sudanese people and leaders of their revolutionary movement were hosted and supported by the Congolese people and their government. South Sudanese responded in kind by extending assistance to Congolese refugees during a series of civil wars that ravaged their nation later.

Today South Sudan is an independent nation, and her people should seek to strengthen bilateral ties with the Congolese people and their government who helped them in their hour of need and do so without meddling in their internal affairs. If these two rich nations become friends, they will learn a lot from each other and help each other while living harmoniously for their common good and for the general welfare of the region. We should thank God that the two nations have never been in bad terms and pray that they will strengthen their relations even more.

South Sudan-Uganda border: As is the case with our border with Congo, we have many ethnic groups which live on both sides of our border with Uganda. Examples include Acholi, Madi, Kuku and Kakwa. This ethnic bond alone if appreciated and exploited in good faith would promote and strengthen our relations for the benefit our two countries.

Because of their geographical proximity, ethnic groups that straddle their two borders, these two states have been assisting each other for long, especially by hosting each other's refugees during civil wars. For example, Uganda became like home for the Southern Sudanese during the last two wars with Sudan. On the political and diplomatic front, Uganda fully participated in all the regional talks that led to the historic signing of the Addis Abba Agreement that ended the seventeen-year civil war with Sudan in 1972. It was also actively involved in a series of talks that led to the historical signing of the Sudan CPA (Comprehensive Peace Agreement) in 2005 that in turn set the stage for the declaration of the South Sudan independence in 2011. Also as part of IGAD, Uganda is now actively involved in looking for amicable solutions to the current civil conflict in South Sudan. At the time of my writing, there is a huge number of our refugees and other kind of visitors in Uganda, among whom are businessmen and students studying in Ugandan schools. There are many benefits that our people have enjoyed from time immemorial as a result of their close proximity with Uganda.

On their part, Ugandans, especially business men and women, have taken good advantage of the bilateral partnership between our two nations as an opportunity to expand their businesses. South Sudan has become a reliable next-door market for their goods and services. These Ugandans are ready to do any kind of work they lay their hands on, and this has led to a boost not only to their personal incomes but also to their national economy. These days there are regular flights between Juba and Entebbe, and the road connection between the two countries is also good. At the same time, our South Sudanese residents residing in different parts of Uganda are also helping in the growing of the Ugandan economy through house rents, school fees and medical fees, etc. Ugandans too had sought refuge in South Sudan during the times of civil wars in the past.

There are benefits related to economies of scale that could accrue if these two highly endowed nations could exploit their geographical proximity and ethnic connections to step their cooperation higher.

To conclude, in the name of our nation of South Sudan, we should play our part in removing out of the way anything that could hinder our good bilateral relations or put our cooperation into disrepute. We should diligently work at maximising our peaceful co-existence. We should thank God that the two nations have always been in good terms and pray that their relationships will even become stronger.

South Sudan-Kenya border: Two major communities that straddle this border are the Toposa of South Sudan and the Turkana of Kenya. There has never been any major dispute between these two nations that continue to enjoy brotherly coexistence, and we hope that the same cordial neighbourliness will continue and even improve for the benefit of the two countries and the entire region.

In terms of business, South Sudan has become a significant market for Kenyan goods and services. Today, there are many Kenyan technical experts and all kinds of business people who are working in South Sudan. There are good air and road links between the two nations. Furthermore, the many South

Sudanese who are now residing in Kenya are boosting Kenya's economy through payment of school fees for their children, house rents and medical fees, etc.

On her part, what benefits has South Sudan been reaping from Kenya? The list is quite very long, but let me just point out here some of the major ones. The first benefit has been the hosting of our refugees for a very long time and Kenya's involvement in the peace processes that culminated in the signing of the Addis Ababa Agreement, bringing to an end the seventeen-year Sudan civil war. Kenya was also fully involved in the tricky political and diplomatic processes that led to the signing of the historic Comprehensive Peace Agreement (CPA) in 2005 between the two warring groups in Sudan and that set the stage for the declaration of the South Sudan independence in 2011. As part of IGAD, Kenya is also now fully engaged in regional talks with the hope of bringing the current civil strife in South Sudan to an end.

Someone might say I am seeing things from the South Sudan perspective and that I don't know the viewpoint of Kenyans with regard to our historical link, but really we South Sudanese highly appreciate the tireless brotherly hand that Kenya has always extended to us. It is our hope that Kenya continues to be a safe haven in the region for the common good of all.

As an independent nation, South Sudan should make sure that our existing good neighbourliness gets better and better for the benefit of future generations.

South Sudan-Ethiopia border: The two ethnic groups that straddle our border with Ethiopia are the Nuer and the Anyuak. This border has never known disputes from time immemorial. And it is our hope that it will remain a peaceful area or, better still, that our relations with Ethiopia will be strengthened even further for the benefit of the two nations and the entire continent of Africa.

In this book I will only highlight a few ways in which Ethiopian people and their government have assisted South Sudan. First is the Ethiopian participation in the political and diplomatic discussions that culminated in the signing of the Addis Abba Agreement, bringing to an end the Sudan seventeen-year civil war in 1972. Second is the hosting and supporting of the Sudan People's Liberation Army and Movement (SPLA/M) by Ethiopia and her people, particularly from 1983 to 1991. Third is the relentless effort made by the Ethiopian nation to bring a peaceful solution to Sudan's problems. The CPA and the eventual declaration of the South Sudan independence were the culmination of those efforts. Fourth is the current involvement of the Ethiopian government through IGAD for a friendly solution to the current civil strife in our young nation. Last, but not the least, is the continued hosting of thousands of the South Sudanese refugees inside Ethiopia territory.

This good bilateral partnership has made it possible for a good number of the Ethiopian citizens to set up profitable business ventures in different parts of South Sudan. They have continued to enjoy the cordial relations and doing business in this young nation and taking back their business gains to boost their home economy.

I don't know how highly Ethiopia rates this bilateral relationship in terms of benefits. But we and our young nation can never forget the assistance Ethiopia has given us over the years. So it is our moral obligation to do whatever we can to step up the level of our good neighbourliness for the common good of the two nations and the region.

Friends Further Afield

I would like us to think of every nation under the sun as a real friend of the new Republic of South Sudan and her people. Our fear and love of God as well as our love for each other gives us and our nation a lot of potential and makes us very important to other human beings, friends or foes.

During our long bloody wars of emancipation, South Sudan received and is still receiving assistance from individuals, agencies and nations from all over the world. This assistance came in material form and sometimes moral and spiritual support. Foreigners of goodwill chose to join and suffer constantly in solidarity with us until some of them unfortunately lost their lives inside our motherland in the process, either through illness or through other causes.

Some nations like USA, Australia, UK, Canada, Norway, Netherlands and New Zealand, just to name a few, took a good number of our South Sudanese brothers and sisters under resettlement programmes. Now they are doing well there, becoming our real ambassadors and strong bridges that connect our young nation with the First World. There are other friendly countries like Egypt, Israel, Tanzania and South Africa, among others, who hosted some of our citizens during and after the war. As I write, some are still living in these countries.

Almost all the peace-loving world nations, including the Arab League, tirelessly pressured the two warring Sudanese parties to get an amicable solution to their problem. These global efforts resulted in the historical declaration of South Sudan as an independent nation on 9 July 2011. The same individuals, agencies and countries mobilised and availed vast resources to kick off the economy of the youngest nation in the world and bridge the wide development gap that has been brought about by the protracted Sudan civil wars. The resources would also lay a foundation from which to launch from as she sets on her path to higher heights of growth and development.

As if that was not enough, the same friends are sleeplessly trying to broker peace between the South Sudanese warring parties so as to put the young nation back on the path of development. They are also working very hard to help South Sudan and Sudan in reaching a consensus so far as their border is concerned and determining the status of Abyei so that the two counties start living at peace.

From the brief outline that shows nations and international agencies that steadfastly stood with us during the war and some until today, it is clear that we South Sudanese owe a lot to other people. We regard all nations of the world to be our friends, including Sudan. Our plea to these people is to be patient with us and continue assisting us until we are past the teething problems of a young nation. Like a baby, our nation will stand and fall, stand and fall until she steadies up and starts moving in the direction of political maturity and socio-economic development.

While people of South Sudan are grateful for the assistance they have received from different parts of the globe, they would like their nation to grow up as a neutral nation with cordial relations with all the countries of the world. Despite that, it is our moral duty not to forget our old friends, even if they deliberately turn their backs on us at some point. Neutrality should be adopted as one of the foundations of our national self-esteem.

Maximisation of Friends and Minimization of Foes

Wise people maximise their friends and minimise their enemies so as to make their life bearable or, better still, exciting. Just as there are friends in life, there are enemies also. You have friends and enemies; I have my friends and enemies. What matters, though, is being able to deal with both difficult and friendly human beings in a way that leads to increased friends and few enemies.

The so-called 'elimination of one's enemies' is a defeatist, inhumane attitude, for no one has ever managed it under the sun. Elimination of one's enemies is like pruning a tree. The more regularly you prune a tree, the more it becomes healthy and produces fruits; likewise, the more you fight your enemies, the more you encourage them to mushroom and increase until they eliminate you in the end. That is why wise people say that if you don't defeat your enemy, join him or bring him to your side. In fact, force creates force. Even God's enemies are still at large, and the D-Day is awaiting them.

Our young nation of South Sudan is likely to make fresh friends and fresh enemies along its rough and twisted path of growth and development. And this is nothing out of the ordinary, especially for a young, inexperienced nation. Some of these enemies will be ready to forgive the wrong and make up, but others will take it to heart and start thinking of ways of retaliating. Our nation is also likely to make mistakes, with bad consequences in the end. Some of her dishonest friends could also entice and drag our country into unnecessary conflicts with other individuals, agencies and nations.

We are familiar with different forms of child abuse that are done by unkind adults. Such may include the use of force to inflict physical damage on the child, use of money or flattering words to influence the child to do wrong, denying the child his rights or subjecting him to heavy work. Similarly, the infancy of South Sudan could be exploited by some unkind, mature nations to humiliate and make her unfriendly to others in the course of achieving their selfish gains.

The noble person or nation under the sun is the one that reaps the consequences of his or her own mistakes. But the worst, humiliated person or nation is the one that suffers the foolish results of mistakes done by someone else, a cunning guy or nation. Each and every person or nation should bear their own cross.

Now what should the young Republic of South Sudan do to maximise her friends while minimising her enemies? There are many things to do but permit me to share just a few of them.

First, our nation should conduct herself very wisely to evade the tricks of those who might want to exploit her vulnerability and grow her economy peacefully and realize her vision as a nation. And this is in line with Jesus' wise words that he told His vulnerable disciples, "I am sending you out like sheep among wolves. Therefore be as shrewd as snakes and as innocent as doves" (Matt.10:16). If we liken our young nation to a disciple and the nations of this world to Pharisees and Saducees, then South Sudan must step wisely, knowing what to do to avoid making unnecessary enemies and maximising her friends among the nations of the world because it needs them for development. Of course, not all the nations of the world are like the biblical Pharisees and Saducees; some are like the Good Samaritan, and we should really cultivate such.

Second, our nation should avoid meddling in other nations' internal affairs. In the same way, our nation should not allow other nations to interfere in her own national issues. May I mention here that our relationships with the other nations should have mutual benefits!

Third, South Sudan must have a strict policy of not paying evil with evil; we should always seek to demonstrate maturity by being good to all, including those who have been bad to us. Even when parting ways with intolerable bedfellows, let it not be done acrimoniously because there may be need to seek their assistance in future. These days we live in a global village that calls for interdependence.

In conclusion, may I share with you a story! The hyena never eats anything from a cattle camp located in the vicinity of its den, reasoning that mourning is not good when it takes place near its children. And I agree with this because wailing near children can have adverse psychological effect on them. Now if a hyena is that wise, how much wiser should we be?

But we should know that this friendly hyena also embraces the dirty policy of eating things that belong to others provided that the owners are living or staying farther away from its hideout. Of course, I really don't know how far away its 'far away' is.

As human beings, we should avoid eating anything belonging to both our near or distant neighbour if we want to come across as being wiser than the hyena. We should have good neighbourliness with all human beings, whether they hate or love us. You may feel obligated to hate me for some reason, but I have a choice to overlook your ill-feelings towards me and love you instead.

Maximisation of friends and minimisation of enemies should be one of the policies that are rooted deeply among the people of the Republic of South Sudan. We should seek to relate well with all people!

Importance of Protecting the Environment

A healthy environment contributes greatly to people's quality of life and national development. A clean environment is a major step in stopping the spread of diseases in any nation. It contributes to people's health and, accordingly, their ability to produce their own food and work in other industries. Healthy people actively participate in the development and protection of their own nation. A healthy environment attracts foreigners, either as tourists or as investors to undertake projects that will be of benefit to the country. It also makes a place worthy to live in or work in.

An unhealthy environment, on the other hand, makes people sick and thus hinders the growth and development of the nation. It also encourages the spreading of diseases. When people become sick and continue eating unhealthy and insufficient food, their life is reduced. But even those who do not die may end up being too weak to actively participate in the development and protection of their motherland. This is not to mention the reduced number of aliens, who fear visiting or investing in such a nation. In short, an unhealthy environment leads to poor people and hence a poor nation.

An unhealthy environment may be caused by, among other things, deforestation where people cut down trees without replacing them; dumping of toxic waste on the land, rivers and other bodies of water; unmanaged disposal of human waste; polluting the air with automobile and industrial exhaust, etc. The list keeps growing.

To have a clean or polluted environment is a choice. It is people who decide what kind of environment they will live in. That is why some houses are clean, while others are filthy. For the same reason, the environment in some nations is clean, whereas in others it is unhealthy. With this awareness, what kind of environment have the people of South Sudan chosen to live in? Do they want a healthy or polluted environment? If they choose a healthy and friendly environment, then they must do the followings, and do it consistently.

First, our administration, from the buma to the national government, should come up with environmental laws or revise the existing ones for effectiveness and enforce them relentlessly and without partiality across the nation. Any violators should face appropriate penalties.

Second, concerted effort to create awareness of the importance of hygiene and clean environment should be made through different forums and the media. Another way of mainstreaming the importance of caring for the environment would be by making it a compulsory subject in schools and coming up with indicators to evaluate progress in pollution control.

Third, we could seek foreign assistance in ensuring that our motherland does not become a dumping ground for expired pharmaceutical products, agricultural fertilizers and chemicals, toxic substances, technical equipment, etc. Even when they are being donated freely, it is better to refuse such goods instead of politely accepting them and soon start looking for ways to dispose them when they have already become an environmental hazard.

Fourth, we should do our best to conserve our natural forests. It is unfortunate that some of our people, and even foreigners, are busy cutting down our trees to burn charcoal. This is tantamount to setting the stage for an environmental disaster, and every effort should be made to arrest this trend before it gets out of hand. Moreover, a campaign should be started to encourage the planting of more trees across the country.

Fifth, dumping industrial and any other form of waste into our rivers should be prohibited and made punishable by law.

Sixth, our people's government should explore ways and means of preserving and protecting our atmosphere from pollution by monitoring the level of industrial waste.

Seventh, all households in urban and rural areas should have latrines and people made to use them always. When people relieve themselves in bushes, their 'droppings' are eventually swept into rivers by flush floods, posing danger to the health of those who drink water from such rivers.

Eighth, since people are the ones who make up the government, all South Sudanese should be required to protect environment where they stay. If you are aware that it is important to keep your house clean, keeping your environment clean is equally important. Indeed, if we don't play our part, we will not have the moral authority to blame the government when environmental pollution eventually sets in.

If we love to live and work in a clean, healthy and friendly environment, we must always play our part in protecting it. Let us keep our urban and rural areas clean and keep our rivers and airspace free from pollution. Also, we should tell our children to tell their children's children that people of South Sudan cherish, uphold and safeguard what makes their nation clean and shun what pollutes it. Respect for our environment should be one of our values and causes of self-esteem. Of course, cleanliness starts in the mind before it is outwardly manifested.

Summary

To enrich our national culture and experience national pride, we should respect human life, senior citizens, the disadvantaged citizens, national leaders, women and the youth and members of the armed forces. We should also respect our widows and widowers, orphans and single ladies and our public wealth. Our individual self-respect should reflect our pride as South Sudanese. We are to respect aliens, our national law, government and politics. To boost our national image, we should share our national cake equitably and promote religious tolerance, forgiveness among our people and good neighbourliness. That way we will maximise our friends and minimise our enemies.

Our collective protection of our national environment is a must if we are to live a healthy life in a healthy nation.

CONCLUSION

There are many moral principles that our people should embrace if our nation is to have a good national foundation. It is upon these that our nation will launch as it takes off as it hurtles down the tricky road of development. In this book, I seek to emphasize the fact that people of South Sudan should build a proper, durable foundation upon which our country is to stand as it moves along the rough path of growth and development. Besides our national principles of justice, liberty and prosperity, I suggest three more moral values: equality, fear and love. These should bring the total of our nation's main core values to six, and they should inform all our national policies, plans and people's ways of life. Our national slogan should be justice for all, liberty for all, prosperity for all, equality for all, fear and love of God as well as our love for one another.

If we exploit our vast national resources and use these principles of justice for all, liberty for all, prosperity for all, equality for all, fear and love

God and our love for each other to guide us in using proceeds thereof, these national resources could become a real national blessing. But if we used the proceeds accruing from exploiting these resources selfishly, these resources will be a curse on us and our nation.

We should bring an end to the present disgracing, national financial scandal in our young nation by forgiving those who might have taken the funds and appeal to those people to return the money and invest it locally in order to invigorate our national economy. In the meantime, we should urgently put in place reliable controls to prevent the ripping off of the exchequer. One of the major wars that South Sudan should now fight and win if it going to develop is that of putting systems in place to facilitate good governance.

In an effort to step up cohesion, we should urgently come up with a unifying, common language of communication among the South Sudanese people. At the same time, we should intentionally fight illiteracy through educational programmes that will involve adults as well as children. If our people have basic education, they will know and defend their rights, prove fit for available jobs, be able to read and understand plans and ways by which they can benefit from them and learn to co-exist peacefully.

The other thing that we should do is to respect human life, be they senior and disabled citizens, national leaders, women and youths, all armed forces, widows and widowers, orphans or single ladies. We should also respect our national resources, both public and private. We should respect ourselves so as to acquire the potential for a healthy respect for aliens. We should respect our national law, government and politics. The other things that will strengthen our nation include sharing of our national cake equitably, forgiveness, religious tolerance, good neighbourliness, maximisation of friends and minimisation of enemies.

For us to experience a healthy national growth and development, we must do whatever possible to make our national environment clean and friendly.

I know there are numerous books on ethics, some picking dust on the shelves and the wisdom they sought to communicate going untold and hence, not practised. But if you read this book and take action, changing your life morally, then its primary goal will have been achieved. In the Bible's book of James we are exhorted to be doers of the Word since that is how we benefit from what we learn.

* 9 7 8 0 6 4 5 3 0 1 0 9 0 *